Learning to Love

Learning to Love

Gretchen Wolff Pritchard

A
JourneyBook
from
Church Publishing Incorporated New York

The following identifies, and gives permissions for, the hymn text citations that preface the eleven parts of *Learning to Love* (taken from *The Hymnal 1982,* Church Publishing Incorporated, New York, unless noted otherwise):

Page 7: "Dear Lord and Father of mankind" #652, 653.
Page 20: "Come down, O Love divine" #516.
Page 31: "My Shepherd will supply my need" #664.
Page 45: "Glorious things of thee are spoken" #522, 523.
Page 53: "Deck thyself, my soul, with gladness" #339.
Page 64: "Amazing grace! how sweet the sound" #671.
Page 73: "People, look East," by Eleanor Farjeon from *Wonder, Love, and Praise,* Church Publishing Incorporated, New York, #724. Copyright Eleanor Farjeon. Reprinted by permission of Harold Ober Associates, Inc.
Page 88: "Light's abode, celestial Salem" #621, 622.
Page 95: "Guide me, O though great Jehovah" #690.
Page 104: "Lord Christ, when first thou cam'st to earth" #598.
Page 113: "Come, labor on" #541.

Other citations:

Page 9: "Now thank we all our God," #533, 534, *The Lutheran Book of Worship.* Used by permission.
Page 16: "Jesus, friend of little children," text by Walter John Mathams. Copyright Oxford University Press. Used by permission. All rights reserved.

Page 22: "Love divine, all loves excelling" #479, *The Hymnal 1940*; #657, *The Hymnal 1982,* Church Publishing Incorporated, New York. Used by permission. (Emphasis added.)
Page 28: Excerpt from "Crossing the Bar," by Alfred, Lord Tennyson.
Page 34: *A Man for All Seasons,* by Robert Bolt. Copyright Robert Bolt. Used by permission of Random House, Inc.
Page 47: *Offering the Gospel to Children,* by Gretchen Wolff Pritchard. Copyright by Gretchen Wolff Pritchard. Cowley Publications. Used by Permission.
Page 59 passim: *Piers Plowman: The B Version,* edited by George Kane and E. Talbot Donaldson. The Athlone Press 1975. Used by permission of the Athlone Press, U.K.
Page 85: *The Man Born to Be King,* by Dorothy Sayers. Used by permission of David Higham Associates, London.
Page 99: Excerpt from "East Coker," *Four Quartets* by T. S. Eliot, copyright 1942 by T. S. Eliot and renewed 1970 by Esme Valerie Eliot. Reprinted by permission of Harcourt, Inc.
Page 108: *The Selfish Giant.* A Reader's Digest Film by Potterton Productions.
Page 121: *Godspell,* text by Stephen Schwartz. Used by permission of Stephen Schwartz.

Every effort has been made to trace the owner or holder of the copyright for every previously published quotation used in this book. If any rights have been inadvertently infringed upon, the Publishers ask that the omission be excused and agree to make the necessary corrections in subsequent editions.

Library of Congress Cataloging-in-Publication Data

Pritchard, Gretchen Wolff.
    Learning to love / Gretchen Wolff Pritchard.
        p. cm. – (JourneyBook)
      ISBN 0-89869-322-5 (pbk.)
        1. Pritchard, Gretchen Wolff. 2. Episcopalians—United States—Biography. I. Title. II. Series.

BX5995.P735 A3 2000
283'.092—dc21
[B]

                                  99-086141

JOURNEYBOOK and colophon are registered trademarks of Church Publishing Incorporated

Church Publishing Incorporated
445 Fifth Avenue
New York, NY 10016

http://www.churchpublishing.org

5 4 3 2 1

for Gwen E. Date

INTRODUCTION

· · · · · ·

WHEN THE EDITORS at Church Publishing Incorporated approached me about writing a book in their "JourneyBook" series, I agreed, "as long as you'll let me write it about doing evangelism with young inner-city children." As Children's Missioner at the Episcopal Church of St. Paul and St. James in New Haven, I was just embarking on an ambitious project under a grant from Trinity Church in New York: I had undertaken to distill the essence of our various programs—all of them still quite new and rapidly evolving—into a methodology that could be replicated by others. I welcomed the invitation from Church Publishing as a spur to the systematic observation and thinking that the work would involve.

I should have realized, however, that in order to write about my present work as a spiritual journey—in order to do what Kathleen Norris describes as "writing from the center"—I would need to begin at an earlier point than the 1995 inauguration of the Children's Mission. As I began trying to write, that starting point continually receded—from my commissioning as Children's Missioner back through my struggles to define and live out my particular vocation (and to balance it with family life), and finally all the way back to my earliest experiences of the mystery of knowing and being known by God.

Tracing my story backwards, I was able to see clearly for the first time how my journey is never the "journey of a soul" in the sense of a single individual: it is inextricably intertwined with liturgy and community. It was my first experiences of both liturgy and community—at seven, eight, and nine years old—that caused the gospel, for me, to leap out of the realm of storybook and rote repetition, and lay claim to my deepest self. And it was the loss and finding again of either liturgy or community or both that have marked the turning points of my journey since then, and shaped what eventually became my ministry.

As these pages will make painfully clear, I am not a spiritual adept. The gift of a vibrant

· · · · · ·

solitary prayer life of meditation and intercession has been withheld from me. Dominated by a restless, hypercritical intellect, I need a visible structure and the company of others to carry me in prayer and praise. When God seems unreal, private prayer or the effort to find God in daily blessings merely makes him seem more unreal (and the growing unacceptability of saying "him" for God has, for me, erased the face of God without replacing it with anything I can relate to). It is in liturgy—the patterned retelling, in community, of God's saving deeds in history; the holding up of permanent, transcendent truths through image, metaphor, and story—that I find myself sustained, drawn out of myself, and able to find the faith and hope that will help me learn to love.

Liturgical spirituality as a path to God has not quite found its place in the recent resurgence of interest in spirituality. It is a particularly Anglican path, yet one for which Episcopalians have recently seemed almost embarrassed or apologetic as our church has tried to stretch in order to appeal to the assumed preferences of a more diverse population. As I have found a clearer sense of my own ministry, I have often felt myself to be swimming against the tide, in trying to offer, to the most marginalized of American children, the riches of Anglican liturgy-in-community that have so nourished me from childhood onwards.

To begin, then: I am a lay person engaged in full-time, high-intensity ministry, based in a parish church but not supported by the parish's budget; rooted in liturgy but (since I am not a priest, and I am working primarily with unbaptized children) not centered in the sacraments. I do some of the things that priests do—including preaching several times a year to the Sunday parish congregation, and quite a lot of guest preaching—as well as all the things that Sunday school leaders routinely do and many of the things that missionaries do. I also do what every leader of a small non-profit organization does: write grants and raise funds in order to keep the organization, and myself, afloat. I have no official credentials in any of the areas in which I work every day. In telling how God has brought me this far (through many twists and turns, and many back doors), I have tried to keep this book from becoming the story of "Why I am not a priest." But the struggle to define a powerful, persistent vocation that has refused to accommodate itself to the usual patterns of either lay or ordained ministry is unavoidably a part of this story.

"No one is ever told any story but his own," says Aslan to the children in C. S. Lewis's "Narnia" series. He is referring to the story of why and how God has given each of us this life—this set of events, opportunities, gifts, temptations, burdens—and not some other. We are to mind our own spiritual business: the only truth we can know without judgment and presumption is the truth about ourselves.

Our own story is notoriously hard to learn with honesty, and harder still to tell with integrity. The only excuse, perhaps, for attempting to tell it at all (besides the selfish one that the telling itself is a form of learning) is the hope that, in hearing it out, others may be led to a clearer knowing and telling of their own stories.

Of the many risks in telling our own stories, one of the greatest is the risk of telling too much or too little of the stories of others. I have chosen, for better or for worse, to tell relatively little, constrained both by space limitations and by the desire to heed Aslan's warning. I have changed or suppressed the names of some places and some individuals. I have also, reluctantly, pruned away from this account much that I would gladly have told of family, friends, and neighbors, if I had had the time and space to do so. I hope those thus underrepresented (you know who you are) will accept, here, my love and gratitude for the grace with which they have surrounded me, supported me, and (too often) put up with me.

As this book took shape, it was blessed with gifts of time, attention, and thoughtful commentary from Susan Amussen, Barbara Cheney, Christen Frothingham, Suzanne

Guthrie, and my husband and two older daughters. In Johnny Ross I have had an editor to die for. And I would not have had the courage to tell this story at all without the examples of Karen Armstrong, Barbara Crafton, Suzanne Guthrie, Kathleen Norris, Anne Lamott, and Nora Gallagher, whose books convinced me that it is possible to write about God, oneself, and the church in ways that are truthful, challenging—even thrilling. Finally, I want to thank, once more, the one to whom this book is dedicated. Would that every child had at least one such teacher.

PROLOGUE

. . . . .

In the summer, when we
came there, I was seven, and the grass was green
and drunk with pears dropped by the dripping tree,
and I squashed them, and all the bees
zigzagged in the golden sun, or stood
delicately twitching on the shiny smashed
sweet sticky wreckage. And I wore
a purple scarf on my shoulders and sang wordless songs
for I knew I was a princess, and I let my hair
hang loose. After the pears vanished into the grass
it was autumn, and the leaves
spiraled slowly into the still cold bottle-green
water in the stone pool under the lion's head—
where seven orange goldfish
darted mysteriously in the darkness, and
stiffened irises guarded the secret
passageway to the cavern where I could look out
the lion's mouth. In the winter
I walked solemnly from school in the lowering
dark, past yellow-glowing shops, to the breathless
quiet at the dark steps by the shriveled hedge, into the silent
garden, and into the house, and cinnamon toast. And then,
when I was helmed and gauntletted,

. . . . .

I rode into the darkness and slew purple leaves, until
the night took hold of me, and numbed
my feet and fingers, and when I came again
into the light, my nose dripped.
I blotted it with the finger of my glove.
In the spring it rained lead, but suddenly
the grass was embroidered with crocuses—
purple, or oranger than fish. And I watched
the pear tree blow blossoms like bubbles, and the sun shimmer
silver through the satin clouds, and suddenly
everywhere there were birds.

In April

I found a naked tiny grey bird dead,
and I buried it near the rim of the stone pool,
and marked its grave with pebbles.
I picked lilac and put it on the grave,
and I was its priest and I was its bard, and I was eight.

. . . . . .

PART ONE

In simple trust like theirs who heard,
  beside the Syrian sea,
the gracious calling of the Lord,
let us, like them, without a word,
  rise up and follow thee:
  rise up and follow thee.

1

THE HOUSE WITH THE PEAR TREE and the stone pool was in London. My father was a Foreign Service Officer; we lived in London for four years. The house was a semi-detached Tudor-Victorian near Hampstead Heath. My parents signed the lease on a sunny day in late summer, when the house's lack of central heating seemed a quaint and trivial concern. There were gas grates and paraffin heaters, but the damp cold in the stucco walls sucked the warmth out of everything inside the house, and all of us were sick all winter. My brother and sister both got asthma; my parents got pneumonia. I was the least troubled by it all, but I too coughed all winter.

In the other half of the house, the mirror image of ours, there is a family with two girls our age. As we are moving in, they stick their heads out the upstairs window and introduce themselves. "We're in quarantine for mumps, but we can come out tomorrow. And Mummy's going to have a baby any day." Within a week, we are great friends, putting on plays and dashing in and out of the two houses, up and down the stairs and around the garden. The baby is born at home, and the morning after his birth, we all troop through the house to see him. Every day, whatever the weather, he sleeps in his pram,

. . . . . .

parked in the front garden. His cheeks are as big and round and red as apples. His name is Timmy, and I adore him.

We go to St. Christopher's School, wearing green uniforms and brown shoes. My father teaches us how to tie our ties. The school is all girls, except for a half-dozen little boys, including our brother, in the kindergarten. Everything about the school is strange. We do our work in exercise books; we have different teachers for different subjects; we learn to sew; we do gym in our shirts and our navy woolen underpants, called knickers; we have Scripture lessons and morning prayers. On the first day of school, we line up to go into "hall" for prayers. The teacher hands me a hymn book, like those the other girls have: Songs of Praise, *with an embossed design on its dark blue cover, of two deer drinking from a brook. It is a book, apparently, of poems, each with a number. I have no idea what to make of it.*

Our family was Christian but unchurched. Back home, in Maryland, I had been given a book of *Prayers and Graces for a Young Child.* They were all in verse:

> It's been a happy day, dear God,
> I helped my mother bake a cake
> And played with Mary on the swing
> And watched the ducks swim in the lake.
> It's been a happy day, dear God.

From this book, and from bedtime prayers ("Now I lay me down to sleep") and mealtime graces ("God is great, God is good"), I had drawn the conclusion that, in order to pray, one had to speak in rhyme. Every now and then I tried it on my own. I had some success, but it was hard work.

It was good to learn some hymns. I found that I loved to sing these new rhyming prayers together with other people; this was much better than saying prayers or reading them alone. And the words were tougher and more interesting than almost anything else I had ever read or heard, and the tunes were strong and sober and joyful:

> Now thank we all our God
> With heart and hands and voices
> Who wondrous things hath done
> In whom his world rejoices. . . .
>
> And keep us in his grace
> And guide us when perplexed
> And free us from all ills
> In this world and the next.

The neighbors' children go to Sunday school at St. Stephen's Church. They walk there, by themselves; their parents stay home with the baby. One Sunday they invite us to go along. After that we go fairly often. The inside of the church is big and high and dark. The vicar is a disembodied voice: "who desireth not the death of a sinner, but rather that he may turn from his wickedness and live." There is a book called the Book of Common Prayer *that has all the words in it, if you can learn how to find the right page. But it doesn't matter very much, because very soon after the "death of a sinner," we all go downstairs to Sunday school.*

Sunday school is in the basement, and it makes no sense. The teacher talks about somebody named Pilot, and tells us to draw pictures. Somehow I have missed the story or the explanation; I have no idea who this Pilot is or what the pictures are supposed to be about. There is a boy named Randy, who draws Jesus in a space suit. Scripture class at school is easier to follow, but only after I realize that Abraham is not Abraham Lincoln. It is hard being the only American in my class. Arithmetic in pounds, shillings, and pence is utterly bewildering, and I am furious with Miss Baker when she reads Little House in the Big Woods *to us. "Once upon a time, sixty yeahs ago, a lit-*

. . . . . .

tle girl lived in the Big Woods of Wis-coe-sin," she begins, and looks up; "which is in Canada," she adds, and when I raise my hand to correct her, she will not listen to me.

2

MY SISTER is only thirteen months older than I am. We were always very different. She was quiet, shy, sensitive, bookish. I was bossy, impatient, and temperamental; for me, books were a springboard for dramatic play and making things, rather than an invitation to lose myself in another world. When our little brother became old enough for me to lure him into my projects and pretend games, he became, and remained, my sidekick and best friend.

After a year in Hampstead, we moved. Our new, centrally heated flat, in the South London district of Putney, was on the fourth floor of a large landscaped apartment complex, with curving drives that were perfect for bike riding. For the first time, my sister and I did not share a room. My bedroom, by far the largest of the children's rooms, was also the play-room for all three of us: it held the blocks, the puppets, the electric trains, the dollhouse. I complained about the lack of privacy, but I loved being in the center of things, and I loved the view out the window. There was a huge tree, and behind it what looked like open country, though it must only have been large back gardens. Great flocks of starlings whirled in the evening sky, rising and falling and twittering.

Our brother began first form at a boys' school, where he developed such severe anxiety from daily threats of the headmaster's cane that our parents moved him after only one term. Girls' schools did not use the cane, but my sister and I, almost nine and almost ten, began to live under the shadow of the Eleven-Plus exam. I had no real conception of how, for English children, success or failure on the Eleven-Plus meant yes or no to eventual university study and the chance for a professional career. For us, this ordeal was moot; we would be going back to suburban public schools in the U.S.; we had years of choices and open doors still ahead of us. Though I no longer felt like a visitor in the world of my school, I never fully lost the feeling of foreignness, a kind of cosmopolitan distance, a sense of immunity to the hard limitations of others' lives.

It was not yet fifteen years since the end of the War; damage from the Blitz was still evident in London, and daily life for most families was austere in comparison to the American suburbia we had left behind. At one point our school announced a "silver-paper collection"; we were all to save the foil bottle caps from our milk, and foil wrappers from sweets, to be salvaged for reuse. My mother shopped at the military PX, where American consumer goods were abundant; there were rolls of Reynolds Wrap in our kitchen, and we children used it by the sheet to make pretend swords, crowns, and fairy wands. It had never dawned on me that it was scarce. I marched up to the teacher and announced that I could bring in a whole roll of silver paper. I could not understand why she was neither impressed nor pleased.

3

HYMNS, HYMNS, HYMNS. There was no written order of service at morning prayers; I remember little of what was said, except that it was Anglican, dignified, and traditional. (O Lord our heavenly Father almighty and everlasting God who hast safely brought us to the beginning of this day, defend us in the same with thy mighty power and grant that this day we fall into no sin neither run into any kind of danger.)

Some of the prayers were said by the teachers, some we recited together, kneeling on the bare wood floor, bare-kneed in our wool tunics and long socks. Afterwards as we sat cross-legged on the floor for the day's announcements, our knees would bear the imprints of the floorboards: ridges of whitened, raised, numb skin that had been pressed into the spaces between the boards as we knelt.

. . . . . .

I can remember certain girls standing at the lectern to read, but I have no recollection of what they read, whether it was Scripture or some other form of instruction or inspiration. Nor do I remember any topical prayers—for political or social concerns, or for members of the school community. What I remember are the hymns: solid, foursquare building blocks of faith, supplication, and praise.

At the Name of Jesus . . . Come, labour on . . . I bind unto myself to-day . . . Alleluia! Sing to Jesus! . . . All things bright and beautiful . . . Ye holy Angels bright . . . Come down, O Love divine . . . All creatures of our God and King . . . The spacious firmament on high . . . Loving Shepherd of thy sheep . . . Lord of all hopefulness, Lord of all joy . . . He who would valiant be . . . Glorious things of thee are spoken.

During the school holidays, our family toured England and took two extended trips to the Continent. Sitting in the back seat of the car, the three of us would sing hymns. With our separate worlds of boys' and girls' schools, they were one thing we had in common. Sometimes we remembered to pack our hymn books, but we usually forgot. It hardly mattered. We all knew all the words by heart.

Immortal, invisible, God only wise . . . Now thank we all our God . . . O worship the King, all glorious above . . . Jesus shall reign where'er the sun . . . For all the saints who from their labours rest . . . Holy, Holy, Holy! Lord God Almighty . . . O Jesus, I have promised . . . Fight the good fight with all thy might . . . God is working his purpose out . . . Dear Lord and Father of mankind ("How well you sing a hymn you like!" exclaimed the music teacher one day of this last one, at hymn practice).

And I remember standing at prayers, singing with my whole heart, with my head thrown back, and my sister telling me she was embarrassed, because her classmates snickered at me. I didn't care.

. . . . . .

4

We have just returned from home leave—a whole summer back in the States. School has already opened. The headmistress of the junior school conducts my sister and me to our new classrooms. My teacher is new to the school; she has taught in Australia and been a junior mistress at a boys' boarding school. Her name is Miss Date. There are nineteen girls in the class: Carolyn, Aziza, Nicky, Roseanne, Jackie, Diana, Delphine, Ruth, Elizabeth, Judith. . . . Our room is on the top floor. Aziza is Pakistani; Ruth is Canadian. Most of us are ten years old.

Sometime this year we will take the Eleven-Plus. In order to spare the children's nerves, the date of the test is not announced in advance. Every Friday, we have a practice test: arithmetic, mental arithmetic, reading comprehension, writing. There is "extra work" for the girls who are not testing well. Besides preparing for the Eleven-Plus, we have history, geography, nature study, Scripture, art, music, and gym. We will start French next year; Latin the year after. My brother, three years younger, is already doing French and geometry, and will start Latin next year, at eight. He goes to school six days a week, and has more homework than we do.

Miss Date is a handsome woman; not young, but lean and healthy-looking, with a strong jaw, high color in her cheeks, and bright, smiling eyes. She is interested in everything: fractions, birds' eggs, Australian cowboy poetry, and us. She is sensible and fair, patient with the bewildered slower students, and challenging to the quick ones. She never treats us as her adversaries, and she knows what fun is. She listens with genuine attention to our accounts of the long-drawn-out pretend game about horses that four of us are engaged in every day at break. "Datey is our matey," I chant in the car going home. "Does Miss Date have you say that?" asks my mother. "Of course not," I answer. "Aziza made it up. Now we all say it."

Scripture class: Miss Date is perched on a desk in the front row, facing toward us, her feet on the desk's chair. A lesson on the Parable of the Laborers in the Vineyard has become the springboard for a general conversation about death and judgment, heaven and hell. Hands are up all over the room.

Everybody has an urgent question—some theoretical, some personal and painful—about deathbed conversions, suicides, heathens in foreign lands; about Hitler and dogs and cats. Miss Date listens attentively to each one, and to the wide-ranging discussion that follows. Her own responses are thoughtful, sensitive, and sane. Something deep inside me opens up, as it does at prayers when we sing hymns. Beyond the lively, friendly, attentive face of my teacher is another Face; beyond the eager faces of my classmates is an infinity of space and time and, beyond even that infinity, a burning love that (if only I knew how) I could approach . . . I could reach . . . I could touch, even now: I could know even as I am known.

At home, I begin trying to pray regularly, to express and channel the intense and passionate feelings I now find in myself for God, for Jesus. In another Scripture class, Miss Date mentions the Bible Reading Fellowship. I ask her how I can learn more. She opens her desk and gives me a little booklet. It has a Scripture passage and a prayer for every day of the year. My friends Nicky and Roseanne and I form a secret society. We pledge to pray daily, to set aside some of our pocket money for charity, and to keep each other from falling into sin.

After we moved from Hampstead, we stopped going to church. I did not miss it. Attending Sunday school had not connected me to the sacraments or to parish life, and nothing in my experience of church suggested that morning prayer read by the distant and mysterious vicar was in anyway richer or more meaningful than morning prayers at school, led by teachers who knew me as I knew them. School was my Christian community; I sank my roots deep into Anglican worship in a community of children who learned, played, and prayed together, shepherded by lay women.

5

Late November: my brother and sister and I have just been to a doctor's appointment, where we were all given penicillin shots in an effort to avoid a bad strep infection that is going around. I am at school, playing at the bottom of the schoolyard during morning break, and I suddenly find I cannot

. . . . . .

walk. My legs will not move. I look down at them; they are swollen and dotted with dark red spots. Two of my friends link wrists to form a seat, and carry me up the long slope to the school door. They find Miss Date. She helps me to the sick room. I lie for a long time on the bed in the dimness, until my mother arrives and takes me to the doctor. My legs and feet have swollen so much that I cannot get my feet into my shoes.

I am in the American Army Hospital for eight days. After the first night, the swelling has gone down; I can walk; I feel perfectly fine; but I am being kept for observation. The doctor says I have Henoch-Schönlein purpura, which can have serious aftereffects, including kidney failure. I am in a large, open, pediatric ward lined with beds for about ten children and cribs for a half dozen babies. Parents are allowed to visit for a couple of hours late in the afternoon; the rest of the time we are on our own. Nurses and orderlies come and go, spoon-feeding the toddlers, changing diapers, doing blood tests, wheeling children off to have their tonsils taken out. There is always at least one baby screaming inconsolably. Lying in my bed, waiting for rest time to be over and visiting hours to begin, I keep hearing my mother's voice under the endless sobs and screams—but I crane my neck towards the door and she is not there.

My parents bring me books and games. I teach myself origami with a kit; I even make the "flapping bird." But mainly I am out of bed, and so are most of the other kids. There is a little five-year-old named Jane. She has a cockney accent and insists she is American. I don't believe her. She follows me around, demanding that I read to her, draw pictures for her, and write stories for her. There is no one to make her leave me alone. Within a few days, we have become implacable enemies; an orderly has to pull us apart as I am sitting astride her, punching her. The ward social hierarchy is based on age, and enforced by pushing, name-calling, and fights. At almost ten, I am the oldest, and certainly the strongest. One afternoon at rest time, I am lying in bed. A new boy comes in with his parents. They whisper and tiptoe as they settle him in his bed, trying not to disturb the other children who are supposed to be sleeping. I stare at him. He is easily nine years old; what if he is older than me? After his parents leave,

. . . . . .

I can't stand the suspense. I get out of bed and walk across to him. "How old are you?" I demand, without a word of greeting. "Nine," he says. "Well, I'm almost ten," I tell him. There are several months' difference; my position is still secure.

The ward staff is overworked; the children are often dirty as well as distressed, and one time I step in something slippery on the floor, and look down to find my foot covered with excrement. The nurses let me help them with the babies. "Don't never leave an open diaper pin in the crib, honey," says the one named Captain Leslie. I spend hours hanging over the crib of one little baby, who is awaiting surgery to remove a growth on her lip. Her name is Vicky.

When my parents finally take me home, I cannot sleep. I am overwhelmed with feelings I cannot name or describe. I lie in my bed in my own room, sobbing; I come out into the bright living room, where my father is reading the newspaper and my mother is sewing. "What's the matter?" my mother asks, her voice full of concern. "I miss Vicky," is all I can think of to say.

6

Jesus, friend of little children,
Be a friend to me;
Take my hand, and ever keep me
Close to thee.

Teach me how to grow in goodness
Daily as I grow;
Thou hast been a child, and surely
Thou dost know.

Never leave me, nor forsake me;
Ever be my friend;
For I need thee, from life's dawning
To its end.

. . . . . .

It was my father who drove me out to the Army Hospital; my mother had gone home to be with my brother and sister. As he carried me across the dark parking lot, I was humming "Jesus, Friend of Little Children." "You don't sound very sick," he said, with that studied cheerfulness that parents cultivate. I was trying to convince myself that I was not afraid; I was also (as I partly knew even then) posturing, playing the part of the "Pious Child."

Some small part of that singing, however, was real prayer. So what became of my innocent, passionate devotion to Jesus during the days that followed? Confined in close quarters, left almost entirely without adult supervision, homesick and scared, the children in Pediatric Ward B became savages. My conscience and my inhibitions fell away completely, and I cannot even remember putting up any resistance: when I found I was the oldest and strongest child in the ward, preserving my dominance became my overriding concern. It made no difference that that dominance was never seriously challenged. My posture was offensive, not defensive. Nor can I remember using my position to defend the littler kids from each other, or for any other wholesome purpose. It was pure aggression, utterly unintegrated with my other self that wrote letters to my grandmother, cared tenderly for the babies, made origami, read *Little Women,* prayed passionately in my bed at home, and sang hymns.

Years later, in ninth grade, I saw the movie of *The Lord of the Flies,* and recognized that anarchic world at once. And ever since I was ten, I have known how decent, nice, polite people become such things as concentration camp guards and storm troopers. All they need is to realize that all the rules have changed, and nobody will stop them.

When I got home from the hospital, I told my brother what it had all been really like. He was just seven; to him it made a good story, he thought it was funny—so, in telling him, I played it for laughs: "I got on top of Jane and hit her and hit her and hit her!—Serve her right!—And I stepped in poo-poo in the middle of the ward!—Ewww!"

I never found words to tell my parents.

. . . . . .

7

I AM HOME from the hospital, but I am not allowed to go back to school till after Christmas. My sister has had the idea of putting on a Christmas play for our parents; she has a partly finished script and some costume sketches. With time hanging heavily on my hands, I take over the project.

We were always putting on plays. At school, the teachers encouraged this: some of the plays were initiated directly by them; sometimes, taking note of the dramatic play that was always happening in the schoolyard, they invited groups of children to present their plays formally, for an audience. The year before, the teachers had discovered a large group of girls practicing a nativity play, with much lively argument, jockeying for position, and realistic dialogue. Within a few days, the play was moved indoors, made official, and taken over by the teachers, who assigned parts and announced that there would be no dialogue, only a narrator (using the measured cadences of the King James Bible) and mime. I was the second innkeeper; my role was to wave my hand in refusal as Mary and Joseph approached. There were rehearsals, and the finished product was very satisfying—dignified and reverent. The schoolyard version, however, was more fun.

My sister's script begins with the Annunciation. I am to be Mary, because of my long hair; she will be Gabriel. Our brother, in spite of being a head shorter than me, is Joseph. The two of them are also shepherds. I will be the angel who visits the shepherds; they will then turn round and visit me as Mary. The most exciting thing about the play is that our mother has given me permission to type the script, with carbon copies.

> *Joseph*:   Look, Mary, I see the lights of David's city.
> *Mary*:   That is good, for I am very weary.

We decide to present a carol concert in addition to the play itself. We rehearse every afternoon. It is not clear who is really in charge, my sister or me. There are quarrels and yelling. Our mother remarks that

. . . . . .

we do not sound very holy. On Christmas Eve, our parents are ushered into my room and presented with illustrated programs. The play and concert go off without a hitch, and our parents are visibly moved. Kneeling on the floor in my nightgown and a blue shawl, I tenderly lay my baby doll in the shoebox manger, as my brother solemnly stands over me holding a flashlight as a lantern. O come, let us adore him.

8

THE SCHOOL YEAR is almost over. We are studying the Acts of the Apostles. Stephen proclaims Jesus as Lord, and is crushed to death under stones hurled at him by an infuriated mob. He looks up to heaven and sees Jesus standing at the right hand of God. Not sitting, Miss Date points out to us, but standing: Stephen's Lord is not statically enthroned, but alert and erect, poised and ready to welcome him into glory. Paul travels from city to city, preaching, breaking down barriers between Jew and Gentile, throwing wide open the gates of the kingdom to all of God's children. He is imprisoned and eventually killed. The church learns, first with reluctance and then with joy and conviction, that "God is no respecter of persons"—that all are equal before God, that God's love knows no bounds of race or nation. On fire with the Good News, utterly oblivious to danger and hardship, the church grows because of the preaching and witness of countless martyrs, missionaries, and saints. Now I understand: nothing is more precious than to know Christ and to make him known; nothing more appalling than to deny him or to keep others from his love. The words form in my mind, urgent and utterly unbidden: "I must preach Christ." I tell no one.

. . . . . .

PART TWO

And so the yearning strong,
with which the soul will long,
shall far outpass the power of human telling.

1

WE HAVE RETURNED from England and bought a house just outside Washington; my sister and I are in junior high school. My parents are worried about our brother. His English school, with its policy of pushing boys to their limits, has made him so precocious that a suburban fourth-grade classroom seems ridiculous. They would like him to go to St. Alban's, the Cathedral's school for boys. One entrée to the school is a choirboy scholarship, so my mother takes him for the audition and reports with pride that he did very well. He is admitted to the junior choir. Unfortunately, junior choristers do not have automatic scholarships to the school, so he is in public school after all. He has been placed in a combined fourth/fifth grade classroom; perhaps he won't be too bored. On Mondays and Fridays our mother drives him to the cathedral for choir practice and evensong. The junior choir also sings the nine o'clock Sunday communion service in Bethlehem Chapel. At night, before he goes to sleep, we hear him singing in his room:

O Lamb of God, that takest away the sins of the world . . .

On Sundays, he looks angelic in his purple cassock. He is one of the smallest boys, and sometimes gets to lead the procession, which moves down the center aisle of the crypt chapel to a small choir bay at the rear, where the boys shuffle and fidget during the liturgy. There is no printed bulletin; the congregation is expected to follow the liturgy through the prayer book alone. I read the fine print; I am

· · · · · ·

beginning to see the shape of the communion service. The hymns are familiar, though some of them are to the wrong tunes.

Until we started coming here I had no idea that there was such a thing as communion. I kneel on the rough needlepointed cushion, between the rows of oak chairs. The boys are singing,

> Let all mortal flesh keep silence
> And in fear and trembling stand . . .

At the altar is a Presence; others are going forward to meet it. They will draw near to the incalculably remote and lovely; they will hold out their hands and take it as their own. I am left behind. Someone has made sure to explain to us that in order to receive communion one must be confirmed. I know nothing about how that might come about.

2

I AM IN NINTH GRADE, the last year of junior high. I have had a growth spurt; after a lifetime of being small and skinny I am suddenly big-boned and broad-shouldered, and above average in height. My red hair is waist length. I don't want to cut it, but I don't know what to do with it, so I wear it in a bun. I have friends at school, but I am not "popular." My reputation rests on my grades and my art ability, but there is a group of wildly creative and gifted artists who leave me far behind. They are kind to me, in a condescending sort of way. They draw caricatures of me, with my hair in a bun, and try to get me interested in the Beatles. But I am deeply suspicious of all things adolescent. I refuse to wear nylons or makeup, and when I am alone in my room I sometimes still play with my doll house. My brother and I zoom around the neighborhood on our bikes, imagining we are fighter pilots; we give secret names to all the streets and parking lots. We spend hours in the basement with his electric trains. My sister despairs of me.

My brother has left the cathedral choir. Now, if we go to church, it is at eleven o'clock for morning prayer. We avoid communion Sundays, embarrassed by our exclusion from the sacrament. The cathedral has no parish structure; we are anonymous visitors and would remain so if we came every week for a lifetime. Usually, we sit in the north transept, rather than the truncated unfinished nave with its boxy plywood partition. The rose window over the south transept's balcony glows with noonday sunlight like a great burning wheel, suspended in stillness. Clergy and choir stream by us in procession and disappear into the arched chancel; heavenly music swells and fades, hovering in the colored light. The voice of the dean reverberates through the nave, the congregation answers with a deep, slow, cavernous rumble, like ocean breakers:

> *Minister:* O Lord, show thy mercy upon us.
> *Answer:*   And grant us thy salvation.
> *Minister:* O God, make clean our hearts within us.
> *Answer:*   And take not thy Holy Spirit from us. . . .

> Almighty God, Father of all mercies, we, thine unworthy servants, do
> give thee most humble and hearty thanks for all thy goodness and
> loving-kindness to us, and to all men. We bless thee for our creation,
> preservation, and all the blessings of this life; but above all, for thine
> inestimable love in the redemption of the world by our Lord Jesus
> Christ; for the means of grace, and for the hope of glory. . . .

I crane my neck sideways toward the huge carved crucifix over the rood screen. O Jesus, Jesus, bring me near to thee, make me thine. My Master, my Savior, my Friend. The organ begins the closing hymn. The tune is a familiar one—it belongs to "Alleluia, Sing to Jesus." But the words are new to me.

> Love divine, all loves excelling,
> Joy of heaven, to earth come down;
> Fix in us thy humble dwelling,

. . . . . .

All thy faithful mercies crown.
Jesus, thou art all compassion,
Pure, unbounded love thou art;
Visit us with thy salvation,
Enter every trembling heart.

The cross is gliding nearer and nearer; the singing of the men and boys grows and broadens; the harmony fills in.

Finish then thy new creation;
Pure and spotless let us be;
Let us see thy great salvation
Perfectly restored in thee . . .

They are coming; they are passing right by me. Their faces are alight with the fire of God.

CHANGED from GLORy INto GLORy,
TILL in HEAVEN we TAKE our PLACE,
TILL we CAST our CROWNS beFORE thee,
LOST in WONder, LOVE, and PRAISE.

I am lifted up, up, up on ocean waves of sound. My heart explodes. I am falling through space. O worship the Lord in the beauty of holiness; let the whole earth stand in awe of him.

3

IN MY ENGLISH SCHOOLS, it was taken for granted that anyone who was not Jewish or Indian or Pakistani had been christened as a baby. "Christening," it seemed, was a naming ceremony. When the school guinea pigs had babies, there was a rush to claim the privilege of christening the new arrivals. The names were chosen, and some lucky girl, picked by the teacher, would scoop the furry little baby out of the hutch, trace a cross on its forehead, and announce, "I christen thee Jocko," or "Brownie," or whatever the name might be. I knew I had not been christened, because unlike my friends, I had no godparents. I assumed that this particular experience had simply passed me by, and that was the end of it.

By an odd coincidence (perhaps there was something to this christening business after all), there was a confusion about my name. My "real name," the name on my birth certificate, was Margaret. But I was never called anything but Gretchen, a German diminutive of Margaret. In England, "Gretchen" was considered outlandish. When I told my name, I got funny looks. Perhaps people were bothered by the name's German origin; perhaps it was simply unfamiliar. In any case, I came to dislike my name, and from time to time I tried to get my family to call me Margaret. It never worked. Indeed, "Gretchen" began to appear as often as "Margaret" on official documents such as medical records and school registrations.

Ninth grade; spring vacation is approaching. Our parents have told us that we will be traveling to Chicago for Easter, to visit our grandfather, uncles, aunts, and cousins. We are pleased; it's been several years since our last visit. These trips are lots of fun. We like our cousins; we love being the guests of honor as we return to the family manse: great aunts and second cousins exclaiming, "The last time I saw you you were this *tall!"; cousins renewing old jokes from the last visit; our grandfather presiding over it all in the huge old house where our father grew up.*

"And while we're there," our mother goes on, "we're going to have you all christened." This is a surprise; we had not talked of it before. Our grandfather is Jewish. Our grandmother, who died before any of us were born, was a Christian Scientist. Both traditions are represented among the great-aunts and cousins. But my father's older brother married a Canadian Anglican, and his younger brother an Episcopalian. Their families are members of the same North Shore parish, and that is where we will be christened.

. . . . .

The idea seems funny: we aren't babies. We giggle, and my sister asks what we will wear. Our mother, deadpan, says she is making us long lacy dresses and frilly bonnets. Actually, she has bought the fabric for dresses and coats: ivory wool for me, pink for my sister. We go shopping for my first heels: plain black calf. I have never worn nylons or lipstick before.

Saturday afternoon: the day before Easter. The family gathers in the chapel of my cousins' church. Aunts, uncles, and older cousins have been apportioned out to us as godparents. The priest begins the ceremony. He asks the questions, and we answer from the book. Then he takes my sister, the oldest, by the hand. "What is your name?" he asks. Shyly, she tells him; he asks again, instructing her to give both her first and middle names. He baptizes her. Then it is my turn. Profiting from her example, I give my first and middle names: "Gretchen Angela." "Gretchen Angela," he says, "I baptize thee in the name of the Father, and of the Son, and of the Holy Ghost." Only later, when my aunt (now my godmother) gives me a small, white morocco prayer book with gold edges, do I realize what I have done. Engraved on the prayer book is my name: "Margaret A. Wolff."

4

WE receive this Person into the congregation of Christ's flock; and do sign her with the sign of the Cross, in token that hereafter she shall not be ashamed to confess the faith of Christ crucified, and manfully to fight under his banner, against sin, the world, and the devil; and to continue Christ's faithful soldier and servant unto her life's end. Amen.

■ ■ ■

WE yield thee hearty thanks, most merciful Father, that it hath pleased thee to regenerate these thy Servants with thy Holy Spirit, to receive them for thine own Children, and to incorporate them into thy holy Church. And humbly we beseech thee to grant, that they, being dead unto sin, may live unto righteousness, and being buried with Christ in his death, may also be partakers of his resurrection; so that finally, with the residue of thy holy Church, they may be inheritors of thine everlasting kingdom; through Christ our Lord. Amen.

■ ■ ■

My brother has also been given a prayer book. He is leafing through it. In the "Collects, Epistles, and Gospels to be used throughout the Year" he finds today—"Easter Even." "Hey," he says, "look at this:"

GRANT, O Lord, that as we are baptized into the death of thy blessed Son, our Saviour Jesus Christ, so by continual mortifying our corrupt affections we may be buried with him; and that through the grave, and gate of death, we may pass to our joyful resurrection; for his merits, who died, and was buried, and rose again for us, the same thy Son Jesus Christ our Lord. Amen.

What a coincidence, we think—that on this very day, the church's prayer is about baptism.

5

EASTER DAY. We go to High Mass at our cousins' parish. The church is crowded, and we find ourselves separated. Music, words, movement, and smells swirl around me. I am detached, almost indifferent; it is too unfamiliar, too overwhelming. And, in a way, nothing has changed: until we are confirmed, we are still barred from receiving communion.

Afterwards, there is brunch at our grandfather's house. I am sitting in the sunporch, surrounded by cousins. On this chilly spring afternoon the sky is white; the sun is struggling to penetrate the cold clouds. I open a gift from one of my aunts: a small gold cross on a delicate chain. It rests on a velvet

. . . . . .

backing in a little hinged box. As I hold it up to admire it, it catches the faint sunlight, and I am suddenly dazzled by a blazing brilliance and have to shut my eyes. In the midst of the redness of my closed lids it still flashes, purple and yellow, a bulging, pulsing cross.

At home, I write a Haiku:

> The small cross flashes
> In the watery sunlight—
> Imprints on my soul.

6

LOOKING BACK, what I remember of this time is a constant sense of longing. I was possessed of a faith of passionate intensity, and had only the privacy of my own spirit in which to express it. At church, I was an outsider. The cathedral had no parish life: no one knew my name, watched me grow, or gave me responsibilities; there was no place to ask questions or learn more; no youth group or confirmation class. At home, we said grace at meals, and kept up the family tradition of Christmas plays into our early teens; but faith was defined as private: it was something you just didn't talk about. And at school, of course, the contrast with my years in England was extreme.

In England, school had been my faith community. There, however awkwardly and (sometimes) perfunctorily, liturgical worship occurred day by day: the cycle of the year was celebrated in a way that invited connections between the natural order, the faith story, personal and communal memory, struggle, and hope. Religious convictions and their implications were visible in the curriculum, and some, at least, of the teachers really cared about furthering the children's growth in faith, and were not afraid to show it. I could not put a name to what was missing in my life, but I knew it was missing. The school's liturgical year was a pastiche of athletic rituals, patriotic commemorations, and Hallmark-driven holidays.

Pep rallies were its principal rite. And I was an exile, yearning for the songs of Zion.

I took my dog for long walks in the small wooded area that bordered the junior high school athletic field. I sat on stumps reciting poetry—especially Victorian poetry about death, which alone seemed able to give words to the longing I felt, to break free of humdrum dailiness and enter into an eternity of light and beauty.

> Sunset and evening star,
> And one clear call for me!
> And may there be no moaning of the bar
> When I put out to sea,
>
> But such a tide as moving seems asleep,
> Too full for sound or foam,
> When that which came from out the boundless deep
> Turns again home.

Adolescent spirituality, like most things adolescent, is embarrassing to experience and embarrassing to remember. I was, inside and outside, awkward, gawky, eager, lonely, secretive, vulnerable, ill-informed, intense, and unbalanced. I wanted to belong; I wanted to be able to talk about God and to know that others felt the same desperate love and longing that I was feeling. I wanted guidance in how to bring this intensity up out of myself and into some kind of action or expression.

My parents have a book, The World's Great Religions *by* Life *magazine. I spend hours poring over it. I am especially fascinated by an extended section in the chapter on Judaism, featuring an Orthodox family with six children. Their life revolves around a daily, weekly, and yearly cycle of celebrations, each with its Scripture, prayers, and traditions. There are rituals for everything: cooking, blessing* food, welcoming the Sabbath, birth, coming of age, marriage, death. I turn to the chapter on Christianity, by far the longest in the book. After a long introductory section with full-color photographs of the Holy Land, medieval cathedrals, and the Sistine Chapel, there are several spreads on the newly formed Church of South India, a merger of various missionary churches, now under local control. A girl is being baptized in a cow trough. A convert sits on the floor of his hut, reading the New Testament by the light of an oil lamp. Peasant women greet each other with clasped hands, saying, "The peace of Jesus be with you." Imagine being able to use such a greeting! Several pages further on, an idealistic young Episcopal priest is shown walking the slum streets of Jersey City. A Catholic nun in a winged wimple squats on the floor of a children's mission, helping a little black two-year-old step into his pants.

I want to be a missionary. I want to do important work for God. I want to marry a minister. We will have six children and we will say family prayers every day. Hidden in the desk drawer in my room are drawings of the children I will someday have.

I turn to the section on the sacraments. Baptism, confirmation, communion. One of the pictures is of confirmation in the Episcopal Church. It is disappointing. Girls are lined up in a blurry row, wearing ugly veils. My friend Karen has told me that she wore a white lace mantilla for her confirmation, and that Bishop Moore leaned so hard into the laying on of hands that she thought he would break her neck. I wish, how I wish, that it would happen to me.

I read the Bible from cover to cover, five chapters a day. When I have finished, I start over. I learn by heart verses—sometimes whole passages—that speak directly to me. Every morning, when I wake up, I read a psalm. I sit on my bed with my bedroom door closed, reading and rereading the baptismal vows in the prayer book that I have now made my own. I read The Robe and The Nun's Story. On Sunday nights, I lie in bed with my transistor radio under my pillow, and listen to the weekly sermon from Dr. George Docherty of the New York Avenue Presbyterian Church. I adore his Scots accent. After Dr. Docherty comes Billy Graham, and then the Salvation Army. I usually fall asleep with the radio still on.

Billy Graham intoxicated me for a while. But Dr. George Docherty answered more of my questions, and filled in some of the gaps in my very haphazard basic instruction as a Christian. Then I discovered C. S. Lewis. I had loved his "Narnia" books ever since I was a child. Now I devoured *The Screwtape Letters* and *Mere Christianity,* and later, in senior high, *Miracles, Surprised by Joy, The Great Divorce,* and the "Perelandra" trilogy. Lewis's tightly reasoned apologetics came along at just the right time, as I was learning critical thinking and syllogistic logic in ninth-grade English class under a highly rigorous (if extremely eccentric) teacher.

Right about this time, also, my parents bought a copy of Robert Farrar Capon's bestseller, *Bed and Board.* I grabbed it at once: a book on marriage by an Episcopal priest with six children, it fed all my adolescent fantasies. Capon was breezy and often funny; his portrayal of family life (insofar as I understood it at fourteen) was highly captivating: earthy, unsentimental, and true to life, yet always pointing beyond itself to transcendent meaning. And even more than C. S. Lewis, he fed my imagination. He helped me name the sense of exile and longing that never left me, and begin to fit it into an articulate theological vision. His embrace of the absurd, his image of creation yearning for the consummation of the heavenly city, his hinting at the shape of the whole scriptural story, all laid the pattern of my own developing spirituality. I was very fortunate. Faith never presented itself, to me, as something to be challenged and outgrown as my intellect matured and sharpened. Always, it was faith that issued the challenge.

My sister and I have taken the bus downtown to the dentist; now we are coming home. The bus drops us at the foot of a long hill; we can either toil up it in the June heat or take a much shorter, though still steep, route through the grounds of the Catholic parish and school, possibly (we have never been sure) committing a grave trespass. We are hot and tired; we decide to take the shortcut. "After all," my sister points out as we reach the top of the parking lot and pass the church doors, "we have a right to be here. We've been baptized, haven't we?"

. . . . . .

PART THREE

. . . . . .

There would I find a settled rest,
while others go and come;
no more a stranger or a guest,
but like a child at home.

1

SUNDAY MORNING in early summer. Wearing high heels, I am stepping carefully down a set of terraced steps through the scrubby woods behind the public library and the junior high school, towards the main avenue where the bus runs. The steps were poorly installed and are badly eroded and full of gravel, dried mud, and litter, and there is no handrail, but the steep driveway of the junior high school is even more perilous in my high heels, and on Sunday morning I really don't want to cut through the Catholic church. I am not going to the bus, I am going to St. Edmund's.

Neither of my parents was available to drive us to the cathedral today. But I still want to go to church, and it has suddenly dawned on me that I don't need anybody to take me; I can just go. St. Edmund's is within easy walking distance, though it would be easier without the high heels. Directly across the avenue, as the hill starts steeply up again, just a stone's throw from the bus stop, St. Edmund's perches on the side of the hill by the entrance to the next subdivision. It is an A-frame, very unassuming; certainly a far cry from the cathedral. I am nervous and somewhat excited. Except for my baptism, three months ago, I have not been to a parish church since I was eight years old.

The church's entrance is at the rear, off the parking lot. The front of the building, facing the road, is a solid wall of glass, divided into random squares and rectangles, with large beams framing the shape of a cross. From the outside, the glass looks uniformly dark. But as I step inside the church doors, the window, a luminous pale blue, completely dominates the space. The huge cross, wine-red, starkly bisects and re-bisects the blue. The varying shades of blue glass are clouded and rippled, barely hinting at the

. . . . . .

31

shadows of the summer trees outside. A plain altar table stands at the center of an open space before the window. The communion rail makes three sides of a square around the altar, with the window as the fourth side. The stalls and pews are blond wood; the small aluminum-framed side windows are plain glass. They are open, with insect screens. There is no air conditioning. The space is full of light and breezes; it instantly gives me a curious but unmistakable sensation of being in a tree house.

One or two of the families scattered through the pews are familiar to me from school; the rest are strangers. The service is morning prayer; I will not be conspicuous. The size and simplicity of the room, the full daylight, and the close proximity of minister and people, stir faint memories of morning prayers at school long ago. The canticles are sung by the congregation, not the choir, as at the cathedral. After some hesitation and mistakes I am able to join in.

> In his hand are all the corners of the earth, * and the strength of the
>   hills is his also.
> The sea is his, and he made it; * and his hands prepared the dry land.
> O come, let us worship and fall down, * and kneel before the Lord our
>   Maker.
> For he is the Lord our God; * and we are the people of his pasture, and
>   the sheep of his hand.
> O worship the Lord in the beauty of holiness; * let the whole earth
>   stand in awe of him.
> For he cometh, for he cometh to judge the earth; * and with right-
>   eousness to judge the world, and the peoples with his truth.

The Lord is in this place, and I did not know it. The Lord is in this strange, light-filled room in the tree-tops; the Lord is in the summer sky and the summer trees; the Lord is in the hearty if somewhat ragged singing of this congregation, and in the swelling vibrations of the electronic organ in the blond wood choir loft behind me.

. . . . . .

O Lord, save thy people, and bless thine heritage.
Govern them, and lift them up for ever.
Day by day we magnify thee;
And we worship thy Name ever, world without end.
Vouchsafe, O Lord, to keep us this day without sin.
O Lord, have mercy upon us, have mercy upon us.
O Lord, let thy mercy be upon us, as our trust is in thee.
O Lord, in thee have I trusted; let me never be confounded.

Picking my way back up the hill towards home, I am almost laughing with amazement and elation. This is church, and it is right here, almost literally in my own back yard. I can come anytime I want. Perhaps I can come to know these people and be known of them. Maybe I can even be confirmed. I feel a tremendous surge of joy and liberation. I have found a home.

2

FOR THE NEXT YEAR, the three of us, or at least my sister and I, walked down that hill to St. Edmund's every Sunday. She and I enrolled in a special confirmation class, along with another senior high student who had also missed the normal eighth-grade preparation. It was taught by the father of my friend Karen, and he used *The Gospel According to Peanuts* as the text. We took it very seriously, attended very regularly, and had, as I recall, some good discussions. We had to pass an examination in order to be confirmed. It consisted of writing out, in full, from memory, the Apostles' and Nicene Creeds and eleven other texts from the prayer book, followed by a ten-minute interview with the rector.

There was a special youth group that fall, for tenth-graders only, led by a young and pretty Mount Holyoke graduate who was engaged to a student at Episcopal Theological

· · · · · ·

Seminary in Cambridge. We met her fiancé when he came down to visit her. I drew an elaborate wedding cake on the *Peanuts* calendar in my room to mark their wedding day. She took us to hear *Messiah* at Christmastime, and I fell madly in love with Baroque music, and asked for the album of *Messiah* for Christmas. The eight or ten kids in the group had a good time together. I fitted in reasonably well; I'd finally cut my hair and begun wearing make-up, and it was a relaxed and friendly group. We laughed a lot and told the same jokes over and over. They got funnier and funnier as the year went on.

There are two thousand kids in the three-year senior high school. The building is enormous and almost brand new. In English class we are reading A Man for All Seasons. *The teacher reads to us from the playwright's introduction:*

> Thomas More . . . became for me a man with an adamantine sense of his own self. He knew where he began and left off, what area of himself he could yield to the encroachments of his enemies, and what to the encroachments of those he loved. . . . [B]ut at length he was asked to retreat from that final area where he located his self. [He was] . . . a person who could not be accused of any incapacity for life, . . . who nevertheless found something in himself without which life was valueless and when that was denied him was able to grasp his death.

Once again it comes sweeping back to me from the Scripture classes with Miss Date: the heroism of the saints and martyrs, the absolute obligation never to deny one's conscience—one's faith—even under torture or on pain of death:

> *Roper:*   Sir, come out! Swear to the Act! Take the oath and come out!
> *More:*   Is this why they let you come?
> *Roper:*   Yes . . . Meg's under oath to persuade you.

· · · · · ·

More:	That was silly, Meg. . . .
Margaret:	But in reason! Haven't you done as much as God can reasonably want?
More:	Well . . . finally . . . it isn't a matter of reason; finally it's a matter of love.

. . . and the strange, simple sentence that had formed then, unbidden in my mind: "I must preach Christ." Every thought, word, and deed becomes heavy with eternal significance. I examine my conscience. I try to fast. I listen to Billy Graham under my pillow, and pray passionately. There is so much I do not understand. I want to know God more and more deeply. I want to witness to my faith. I have no idea how to begin.

3

THERE IS A GROUP OF GIRLS *at school who go to Teen Breakfast Club at Fourth Presbyterian Church. They are all pretty and popular, have shiny hair, and smile radiantly all the time. They have bubbly handwriting and pass notes in class that always end "In Him," or "In His love." They are never awkward or uncertain. Jesus is their best friend, and they are always ready to talk about the happiness they feel in knowing his love. I watch them hungrily from a distance, and they start to notice me. They go out of their way to be nice to me, even though I am from a different crowd—the intellectuals, who are mostly Jews and Unitarians. Debbie, one of their leaders, invites me to come to TBC. My parents give permission, and I set my alarm for six o'clock and walk to the church before school. The room is full of kids—boys as well as girls. Church ladies are serving pancakes and sausages. Chuck, the youth minister, stands at the microphone, pumping his arms like a drum major. Everybody is singing at the top of their lungs. The song has the rhythm of a fight song.*

. . . . . .

I am the resurrection and the life!
He that believeth in me, though he were dead,
Yet shall he live,
Yet shall he live!
And whosoever liveth and believeth in me
Shall never, never die!

Chuck takes the microphone and asks everyone who loves Jesus to stand up and cheer. Like everyone else, I leap to my feet. Tears come into my eyes. At last, here are people who are not embarrassed to declare their faith, their love for their Lord. I tell my mother that I want to start going to TBC every week. She is alarmed, and calls the rector of St. Edmund's. He backs her up, with some choice words about Chuck and his influence on the kids at the high school. I am baffled and upset: I can't understand why they are objecting.

"At least wait until you've been confirmed," my mother says. "You're only just starting to be an Episcopalian, and now you want to go to this thing at the Presbyterian Church." She doesn't understand. It's not about Episcopal or Presbyterian; I couldn't care less about the difference between Episcopal and Presbyterian; in fact I am completely ignorant of the differences, if any, between Episcopal and Presbyterian. My mother says something about "fundamentalists." I don't know what they are, either. All I want is to be with people who love Jesus.

Then I realize: it has happened to me. I am being persecuted for my faith. I resolve to suffer valiantly. I tell the TBC crowd that my parents won't let me come. They are effusively sympathetic, and promise to pray for me. But I can't help noticing that they have stopped going out of their way to be friendly.

. . . . . .

4

IN MAY, THE BISHOP came for confirmation. I was disappointed that it wouldn't be Bishop Moore, who was tall and craggily handsome and leaned so strongly on the heads of confirmands to impress them with the gravity of the promises they were making. I sat in English class daydreaming and drawing pictures of myself wearing the hyacinth-blue voile confirmation dress that my mother was making for me, and the white lace mantilla my grandmother had sent.

We are seated in the front pew: the three senior-high confirmands and a sizeable group of eighth graders. The rector has warned us that the bishop may, during his sermon, address us directly, and if so, we are to stand respectfully. The sermon passes without incident, and the bishop steps down from the pulpit to take his seat. He is soberly vested, with full white sleeves and a purple satin sleeveless tunic, heavily creased with a pattern of folds from the suitcase in which he carried it here. He does not have a miter or a staff. The first two kids come forward and kneel side by side before him:

"Defend, O Lord, this thy child"—his right hand arcs gently downwards onto the head of the first boy—"and this thy child"—his left hand comes down and rests on the head of the other—"with thy heavenly grace, that he may continue thine for ever..." Oh, so that's why we are paired off, boy with boy and girl with girl: the bishop wants the prayer to be in the singular, even though he is efficiently confirming two at once. It sounds odd, though. Now it's my turn. I'm on the bishop's left. "Defend, O Lord, this thy child," he intones, "and this thy child," and I feel his hand resting lightly on my white lace mantilla—"that she may continue thine for ever; and daily increase in thy Holy Spirit more and more, until she come unto thy everlasting kingdom."

It's done. I have arrived at last. But the consummation is still one week away. The following Sunday will be our first communion.

Sunday after Ascension. My sister and I are again wearing our confirmation dresses and mantillas. The other confirmands are scattered throughout the congregation, with their families, but we have misunderstood the rector's instructions and are kneeling apart, alone in the front pew. I am distracted by hunger: I told my mother I wanted to fast, and she understood and did not make me eat breakfast. My head is bowed over my tightly clasped hands. It is coming, the moment I have awaited so long, with so much secret midnight agony. O Lamb of God, that takest away the sins of the world, have mercy upon us. O Lord I am not worthy. O Lamb of God, I come. The wafer is in my cupped hands: hold infinity in the palm of your hand, and eternity in an hour. The wine is in my mouth. Its powerful sweetness staggers me. I will never be the same again. It is full springtime; the world blazes in dazzling blue and gold, the peace of God which passeth all understanding.

At home, I sit at the kitchen table, devouring the scrambled eggs my mother has cooked for me. I am ravenous, but I am full, full, full to overflowing. My cup runneth over.

5

JUNIOR YEAR. We are no longer going to St. Edmund's. My parents want to attend church with us, but could not get used to the modern architecture at St. Edmund's, so we have transferred to Trinity, which is Gothic, with stained-glass windows, crimson carpets, air conditioning, a men-and-girls choir at nine o'clock and a men-and-boys choir at eleven, and many, many more members. The youth group, known as the Episcopal Young Churchmen, is huge. My sister has no interest in it, but I want to belong; I have been formally inducted into it and am trying to make some friends. The kids all seem to have known each other since they were in kindergarten, and hardly any of them go to my school. The meetings are led by the assistant minister and several adult leaders. There is an organized discussion or program, and then they bring in Coke by the case. Teenagers are supposed to like Coke, but I don't, much. The discussions are about parents and getting along in school, or feelings, or sometimes civil rights, or the Vietnam War, or the protest movement. Once, we see a movie, Little Boxes on the Hillside, which tells us how suburbia has made everybody who lives in it come out exactly
. . . .

the same. I am bored. I keep waiting for the discussions to be about God, but the leaders seem almost apologetic about the fact that this is church, and in awe of the teenagers, as if we were somehow purer and more honest than they are.

Some of the boys are very cute. David is a senior, and gorgeous, with a Kennedyesque shock of blond hair and a lordly manner. He is obviously an intellectual, and an expert at playing on the adult leaders' sense of unworthiness. He makes arrogant and provocative remarks about the church, the nation, and our parents' generation, and enjoys watching the assistant minister squirm. Bart is a junior, very quiet and deep, tall and skinny with gentle brown eyes and long hair that he tosses back with an adorable flick of his head. He carries the cross in the procession on Sunday mornings. Once, in the hall, I overhear him talking to another kid. "You see, he loved us so much that he could even say, 'Father, forgive them, for they know not what they do.'" He is talking about Jesus. I am undone. But he never once looks at me.

In spite of my efforts I remained a complete outsider in the group: hardly anyone ever spoke to me. I kept coming to meetings almost until graduation, and even went on a memorable "retreat" where the boys found their way into the girls' sleeping area and somebody passed around a mouthwash bottle full of gin. My parents invited the assistant minister to our house to explain how this had happened. By senior year I had found a different niche. I volunteered to help with the Christian education program and was assigned to Mrs. Neill, who ran the three-year-olds' nursery during the nine o'clock service. Cathy, the other teenaged helper, picked me up at home in her own little red car, and I stayed right through to attend the eleven o'clock service with my family.

I had done some babysitting, though not as much as Cathy. The work was easy, and I fell in love with several of the children—Stevie because he was bright and redheaded and British, Betsy because she fell in love with me. But I was surprised to find that there was no religious content in the nursery. The children said "God is great, God is good" over their juice and graham crackers. That was all. At circle time, Cathy led them in songs like "The Wheels on the Bus." I asked Mrs. Neill if I could introduce a short worship service, and when she gave me permission I worked hard devising what I thought would be a simple, age-appropriate order. I would have the children sing a hymn, then say the Lord's Prayer and one paragraph of the Creed: *I believe in God the Father Almighty, Maker of heaven and earth, and in Jesus Christ his only Son, our Lord.* Then I would say a closing prayer.

The children are all sitting on the floor around me. We have sung "Jesus Loves Me," and said the Lord's Prayer. Some of them are clearly lost and confused; others are still with me. "Now," I announce brightly, "we're going to say the Apostles' Creed." There is an audible gasp from Mrs. Neill, and I hastily turn to her. "Just one sentence of it," I explain. But in turning to her, even for a moment, I have lost the kids. I push on. One or two of them successfully repeat the words after me. Mrs. Neill shushes them for my closing prayer. Afterwards she thanks me, and suggests that next time I should shorten the service to just the hymn and the Lord's Prayer. I can hear her and Cathy chuckling together. They are both really nice; they don't intend to be mean. But they think I'm crazy. Everybody thinks I'm crazy. Maybe I am crazy.

6

LINDA SITS BEHIND ME in the eleventh grade "Rapid Learner" English class. She plays violin in the school orchestra, does volunteer work as a Candy Striper at the hospital, and belongs to a Methodist church. We eat lunch together, and become good friends. She lives in a small tract house and is not part of the intellectual crowd. She has the use of her parents' aged VW bug; she takes me hiking near Great Falls and has taught me how to ice skate. I have introduced her to the cathedral. We go to evensong, and save up our allowance for concerts by English boy choirs and early music ensembles. We haunt the cathedral bookstore: it's there that we have discovered many of the C. S. Lewis books. Like me, Linda

. . . . . .

has a secret life with God. We sit together at lunch and talk about what we are reading. Our talk is headlong and excited; we look eagerly into each other's faces; but always the moment comes when we stumble and grope for words, gaze away, and fall silent. The untouchable holiness of the One we both love, at once unites us and separates us.

■ ■ ■

The TBC crowd and their youth minister, Chuck, have become the center of a storm of controversy at school, for the aggressiveness of their evangelism and their arrogant attitude towards Jews. At a student government election assembly, one of the candidates whips himself into a frenzy, bellowing, "... and I will not allow this school to be taken over by anyone, whether it's Chuck Mitchell or Mao Tse-tung!!" I am no longer tempted by TBC. I'm now a communicant, and I have Linda. I have come to realize that I will never enjoy pep rallies, even pep rallies for Jesus. And Jesus isn't my best friend. Jesus is my Lord.

■ ■ ■

Linda and I are at a choral concert at the cathedral. There is a contemporary piece, called "Changes," based on English bell ringing. The text of the piece is a collage of Scripture, traditional children's songs and rhymes, and mottoes from English church bells. One of the mottoes forms a clashing, strident refrain: Vae mihi si non evangelisavero! "Woe unto me if I proclaim not the gospel!"

VAE MIHI SI NON EVANGELISAVERO!
"I must preach Christ."
Woe unto me if I proclaim not the gospel!
How, Lord? What are you asking me to do?

■ ■ ■

I am applying to colleges. I write my essays about the contrast between English and American schools, and pore over college catalogs, trying to imagine living in a dorm, going to college classes, choosing among so many subjects . . . finding a new church. Some of the catalogs make mention of religious *life on campus, or include lists of local houses of worship among the information at the back of the catalog. Sitting on my bed with the catalogs in my lap, I daydream: I might be going to this church; I might find a truly deep and meaningful Christian community here. Visiting colleges during the summer, I peer out the car window as we approach the campuses and drive away from them. Maybe I can spot the Episcopal Church. Of course, I say nothing about this to anyone.*

Wellesley has a large and exciting-looking department of religion. But there would be no sense in majoring in religion. People would think I was weird, and anyway, what could I do with it? Girls can't be ministers. Besides, maybe the faculty are all followers of the "God is Dead" movement that has been in the news so much lately. Sometimes I wonder if Linda and I are the only people left, besides fundamentalists, who still really believe the Apostles' Creed. Bryn Mawr has no department of religion. This is part of its austere and scholarly style; it also has no studio arts or performing arts for credit. It has just begun building up its history of religion department, but no major is available. By the same token Bryn Mawr has no chapel and no on-campus religious life, only an interfaith association that sponsors discussions. Come to think of it, that might simplify matters; I wouldn't have to choose between two competing communities, and anyway, if a campus chaplaincy is interdenominational, or anything like the youth group at Trinity, I would probably not be interested in it. I'm really not part of the youth culture; what I want is Episcopal liturgy. I'd rather be in a parish. I want to teach Sunday school.

7

EVERY DAY, the Vietnam War fills the evening news. American soldiers are dying; Vietnamese children are being burned alive by napalm. Martin Luther King calls for rededication of our nation to peace and economic justice as well as integration. Protesters pour blood on draft records. Eugene McCarthy is running for President on a peace platform. McCarthy buttons sprout everywhere at school. President Johnson announces he will not seek reelection. Martin Luther King is shot in Memphis. In a paroxysm of helpless rage, rioters smash, loot, and burn their own neighborhoods in Washington and dozens of other cities. Our school's senior prom is moved from a downtown hotel to a country club far out in the suburbs. Protesters shut down the Columbia campus. The assassination of Robert Kennedy occurs just before our class graduates from high school. Exhausted and cynical, we file into the field house on graduation night. Our class has decided to abolish the ceremonial roles of valedictorian and salutatorian. This is a protest against elitism. Instead, the opening and closing speeches are given by the class president and vice president. The speeches have a common theme: relief that we are out of here, that we will soon be through with foolish rules and labels and adult interference, and freer to change the world.

The peace movement flooded me with guilt and confusion. I was not political by temperament, and as a diplomat's child I was profoundly and permanently uncomfortable with the simplistic self-righteousness of the anti-war slogans. Of course "War is not healthy for children and other living things"; who could seriously dispute such a statement? So why parade around with picket signs proclaiming it? Whom were we fingering, whom were we demonizing, by implying that they would dispute it? And what kind of intellectual honesty was it, to take refuge in such platitudinous slogans, when clearly the real question lay elsewhere: whether war, unhealthy as it is, might still be necessary, in order to defend and protect something precious that would otherwise fall victim to aggression?

But how to know if this was such a case? I was far too thoroughly shaped by the Book of Acts and *A Man for All Seasons* to be able to take up a picket sign or hand out a leaflet unless I was certain beyond a doubt that I could put my name to the message it bore. I knew I should articulate my own Christian perspective on the war, but I had little trust in the information provided by either side, little basis on which to develop clear, responsible independent convictions, and, to tell the truth, not enough real intellectual interest to spur me

. . . . .

to do the necessary work. I went off to college knowing that if I was not part of the solution I was part of the problem, but paralyzed as to what to do about it.

Maybe when I graduate from college, I'll have found a group of people who are wholly dedicated to living out the gospel and can help me figure out what that really means. We'll sit around a kitchen table, bound together by the power of God's love for all of us and for the people we will serve. We'll plan and organize and pray, and we'll get up from the table to go and do our work, strong and secure in the knowledge that we are doing God's will.

PART FOUR

. . . . . .

See! the streams of living waters,
    springing from eternal love,
well supply thy sons and daughters,
    and all fear of want remove.
Who can faint, when such a river
    ever will their thirst assuage?
Grace, which like the Lord the giver,
    never fails from age to age.

1

WHEN I WAS ADMITTED to both Wellesley and Bryn Mawr and visited both colleges again, I happened to fall in with a much friendlier group of undergraduates at Bryn Mawr than at Wellesley. For this quite trivial and arbitrary reason, I chose Bryn Mawr. In July, the freshman handbook arrived in the mail. It was written by a committee of students and illustrated with cheery cartoons, and it described the student government system, the honor code, the infirmary, local shopping and points of interest, numerous college organizations, and, to my astonishment, a long list of elaborate college traditions.

Parade Night, Step Sings, Lantern Night, May Day, and more: no one had mentioned any of this to me on my two visits. In fact, the years I spent at Bryn Mawr were a period of eclipse for many of these rituals. The countercultural revolution criticized all traditions indiscriminately as part of a frivolous, oppressive, and contemptible old order, and in most circles it was bad form to admit that one enjoyed them or thought they somehow mattered. Only a few years later, they would be rediscovered, as rites of spiritual passage in a feminist

. . . . . .

alternative universe. But in my day they were raggedly carried out and poorly attended, except for Lantern Night in October, when the freshmen and sophomores processed in the dark into the library cloisters, singing, and lanterns were ceremonially given to all the freshmen in the name of Athena, goddess of wisdom. As debilitated as most of the traditions were, however, they provided something in the life of the school that I had been yearning for since we had left England: a framework of communal celebrations (based on something other than competition, sports, and popularity) that was tied to the seasonal cycle, linked the community to its past and its values, pointed to its future, and touched the formative moments in its members' lives.

I had very few clear ideas of what I wanted out of college. I assumed I would go on doing well academically; I supposed I would also begin to sift through the interesting possibilities and start to decide what I really wanted to learn and be. More immediately, I wanted to escape being a complete wallflower socially and possibly even fall in love; to make decisions independently of my parents; and to go to church as often as I pleased, including weekdays if I felt like it.

There are three Episcopal churches within walking distance of the college. Redeemer, in Bryn Mawr, is the closest. It is large, well-organized, and conventional; I am ready for something more interesting. Good Shepherd, Rosemont, is Anglo-Catholic. To walk to it you first pass a stretch of big old suburban houses with deep, shady gardens; then go under a railway bridge and emerge onto a crooked little street lined with tiny row houses that look like picture postcards of England or France. It is a magical transformation—like passing into one of those sugar Easter eggs with a hole at one end and a tiny scene inside. The church is beautiful, delicately proportioned, set in a carefully tended garden. It is fascinating, but I can handle it only in small doses. By now I have made a friend, Ann, who is also an Episcopalian and looking for a church. When we find St. Mary's, Ardmore, we know we can stop looking.

St. Mary's is almost two miles away, closer to Haverford College than to Bryn Mawr, a much

· · · · · ·

longer and less pleasant walk than Redeemer or Good Shepherd. For a while, Ann and I take the train (two stops on the Paoli Local); later, we find a ride with a faculty couple. The parish is integrated, slightly unbuttoned, lively, full of children, a little trendy, and unabashedly and winningly friendly and sincere. I have never seen girl acolytes before; I have never been invited to tea by a feisty old lady who refers to Ann as my "sidekick" and tells stories about playing hockey at Wellesley in 1910. She is bemused by the bearded young curate at St. Mary's. "He congratulated me for being liberal," *she says.* "I told him, 'Why *shouldn't* I be liberal? I've been liberal *all my* life!'"

2

CHURCH WAS FUN, and it was there I took the next shaky steps into Sunday school teaching that I have described in my book, *Offering the Gospel to Children:*

> As a sophomore in college, I decided I wanted to teach Sunday school. I called the parish office, and was put in touch with the assistant, a young man a couple of years out of seminary who had just arrived that summer. He was thrilled to hear that I wanted to teach. He assigned me to the second grade, showed me where the classroom and supply cabinet were, and turned me loose.
>
> I knew nothing about second graders. I had no curriculum. I had been in the parish less than a year, and I knew none of the children and none of their parents. I had no idea what they had done in their previous year of church school . . . it never dawned on me, all year, that teaching primary children might require different methods than the college-style lecture and "discussion" I was using. I did keep order in the classroom, more or less.

Ann and I taught Sunday school during the nine-thirty service and stayed for the eleven o'clock. St. Mary's was not a campus parish, though a number of faculty and staff from both

Bryn Mawr and Haverford attended. We were, as far as we knew, the only undergraduates in the congregation. The preaching was not intellectual in style, nor was our student world addressed at all in the parish activities. I am not sure the rector ever learned our names. But the new assistant who arrived the summer after our freshman year turned out to be the young man who had been engaged to my tenth-grade youth leader at St. Edmund's. They now had a small daughter and were expecting a second child. Ann and I became their regular babysitters.

Church was our foothold in the prosaic ordinariness of family and civic life, a weekly dose of the "real world" in welcome contrast to the campus's isolated, homogeneous intellectual and political hothouse. This was a complete reversal from my school years, when church (even St. Edmund's) had been for me a transcendent realm of unchanging and majestic language, a place to draw near the burning bush and fall down in awe. Not only at St. Mary's, but all over the church, the beauty of holiness was going out of style.

Burlap banners and dialogue sermons replaced canticles sung in Elizabethan English as mainstays of Episcopal worship; the long process of prayer book revision made for years of self-consciousness and gaucherie. When the 1967 "new liturgy" was introduced during my last year of high school, I had been immensely relieved to find that it did not embody modernist revisions of Christian doctrine or suggest that God was dead. I then found I was elated to be given new words and forms for affirming old truths—to be invited to greet my neighbor in Christ's name; to be impelled to learn all over again how to pray and praise, as the framers of the first prayer book intended, "in a tongue understanded of the people." Later I would also realize how much scholarship lay behind the revisions, and how much ancient liturgical theology was brought back to life in the 1979 prayer book that eventually resulted from the process. But in the short run, the constant experimentation and flux were tiring, and the church's movement away from the solemn and transcendent towards the immediate, the topical, and the personal became, for me, a serious impediment to common prayer. Now and then I sought an antidote at Good Shepherd, but the Anglo-Catholic ritual there was forbiddingly arcane. I was simply not an initiate.

I enjoyed the homey fellowship and relaxed attitude at St. Mary's. They spoke to me of love and care. But I was beginning to find that they did not, for me, point towards a deeper experience of God. That came from somewhere else entirely, which I had not anticipated at all.

3

MY PROFESSORS in the English department would probably be shocked at the idea that in their lectures and seminars on Chaucer, Shakespeare, Spenser, I encountered some of the best *preaching*—the best application of text (including scriptural text) to the crucial questions of human life—that I have ever heard. Courses in history of religion, history, and medieval art stitched back together for me the fabric of Western intellectual history that had been torn apart by six years of public secondary school and the secularist, pragmatic popular culture. I had been worried that what I would learn in college would challenge my faith, and force me to wall it off from my intellect. I felt I was taking a calculated risk in signing up for "Introduction to Biblical Literature" with Howard Kee the first semester of my freshman year. I found there was nothing to fear, and this discovery was enormously liberating.

And in this small college, it was possible for someone like me, who had never before sung in a choir, to try out for the college chorus and be thrown straight into the deep end of Bach's *Magnificat* and Stravinsky's *Mass,* to sink or swim. I very nearly sank, but after two or three semesters I was swimming. We did *Israel in Egypt,* the *B Minor Mass,* Hindemith's *Requiem,* the *St. John Passion.* I moved from class to chorus rehearsal to library to study to church and back again, soaked in poetry, music, and prayer. Fed by such springs of living water, my inner life became a lush garden, almost unbearably fertile and tender—and private, hidden, surrounded by high walls.

College life is artificial and intense. Many of us never left the Bryn Mawr campus except to travel back and forth to Haverford, then still an all-male college, one mile down the road. Even in the midst of the ferment over Vietnam and the draft, the two colleges were leafy and lovely and almost completely isolated from the outer world. There were students who were genuine activists, taking part in peace marches, political campaigns, and teach-ins. There were others for whom the revolution consisted only of sexual emancipation, casual drug use, and a contempt for authority that was at once cynical and naive. And there were plenty, myself included, who more or less sat out the entire movement. I made a few efforts to translate my faith into action. For a while I volunteered at a children's center in Philadelphia on Saturday mornings, along with a group of other students. Then the city closed the center, and I did nothing more for a long time. Activism, rather than direct service, was the order of the day, and activism was simply not my style.

I lived all four years in the same residence hall, as did many of my friends. The old dorms (ours was built in 1912) were homey and comfortable. Until my senior year, meals were served family style, in one sitting, in the dining hall of each dorm. Announcements, birthday greetings, and occasional ritualized jokes punctuated the meal. The long, wide corridors lined with single and double rooms encouraged genuine community life. Both solitude and company were available, in good proportion; there was seriousness and fun, and the hard and important work of learning to live with others when none of us was always at her best. We had our share of ennui, adolescent and romantic despair, complaints about the food, feuds over loud music and lifestyles, and stress: we were busy; there was intense academic pressure and always more work to do than time to do it in. Never having lived on our own, we did not sufficiently appreciate how community living simplified the mechanics of

· · · · · ·

life—meals, laundry, shopping, daily tasks—leaving room for reading, thinking, learning, conversation. Weighed against the life many of us would be leading a few decades later, the undergraduate years now seem wondrously spacious and serene. And brief.

4

I DID NOT REALLY BEGIN to date till I went to college. My parents had been markedly nervous about dating, parties, boys, cars, and the whole rest of the high school scene, and I had welcomed their restrictions and, I suppose, projected a fairly intimidating image to most high school boys. I was surprised to find when I got to college that I had plenty of invitations, and sometimes even the heady experience of juggling two or more prospects. I met Arnie at the "College Sunday Luncheon" at the Church of the Redeemer in September of my sophomore year. The long-suffering church ladies had invited Episcopal students from all the local colleges, and set places for eighty. Seven actually turned up. Arnie was a junior at Haverford, with cowlicky hair and soft brown eyes. He walked me back to Bryn Mawr, and turned up the next day at lunch in my dorm. He pursued me doggedly even when faced with a formidable competitor—the big brother of my second-best friend, a law student with a Harvard degree, a car, and a fondness for expensive restaurants. Arnie won, and we were "getting serious" by spring of that academic year.

I was attracted to Arnie for his intelligence, his complete trustworthiness and decency; his seriousness of purpose and (not least) because he thought I was beautiful, interesting, and smart, and said so. We were both church-going Episcopalians in a campus atmosphere where explicit religious faith was rare and consistent religious practice almost nonexistent; we were steady and studious and fairly comfortable with traditional values at a time when "tuning in, turning on, and dropping out," or at least radically questioning almost everything, seemed to be the rule.

· · · · · ·

Haverford, in particular, had a reputation as a nest of bearded, unwashed, arrogant, and self-absorbed peaceniks. The reality, not surprisingly, was a great deal more complex. Both colleges had been founded by Quakers, but Bryn Mawr was robustly, even aggressively, secular: its institutional religions were scholarship and an austere and cerebral feminism. At Haverford, the language of peace, of non-violent conflict resolution, of respect for individual conscience, was much more than a collection of slogans. It had a depth born of generations of patient discernment in community, and formed a palpable spiritual bond between the institution and its students.

I had no real appreciation for the gravity of the questions facing Arnie and other males as they neared graduation. I was a year younger and, growing up as a girl in a family where my father was the sole breadwinner, I had not gone to college with any clear expectation of preparing for a professional career. Nor had I had to confront my own conscience in the face of a letter from the Selective Service. My world was made up almost entirely of literary and aesthetic imagination and unfocused spiritual intensity. I listened sympathetically as he agonized over career choices and whether to apply for conscientious objector status. None of it seemed real.

Arnie exempted out of the draft thanks to a benign heart murmur and a knee injury, graduated, and went off to Yale to begin work on a Ph.D. in history. I spent my senior year doing Greek, seventeenth-century English poetry, and an honors paper on medieval English religious lyrics that filled me with rapture. Arnie's letters from Yale were restless and unhappy and beginning to hint of the coming disaster in the academic job market. I applied to the English Department of Yale Graduate School to be near him and because I had no other ideas about what to do next.

· · · · · ·

PART FIVE

Jesus, Bread of Life, I pray thee,
let me gladly here obey thee;
never to my hurt invited,
be thy love with love requited.

1

IF I HAD BEEN MALE, I would almost certainly have decided, probably in my early teens, that what I wanted to do when I grew up was to be a priest. I would presumably have mentioned this at some point to some clergyman—I had become acquainted with nine or ten by my last year in college—and been encouraged to feel that I was embarking on an exciting, serious, and important quest. I might have been offered spiritual advice and direction, and encouraged to apprentice myself to a mentor within the church. It is harder to guess what I would have done, as a woman, graduating from college in 1972, if the Episcopal Church had fully opened ordination to women in, say, 1970 instead of 1976. I still might not have taken my own spirituality and my own vocation seriously enough to overcome my conditioning and envision ordained ministry for myself.

I was not brought up to be a pioneer. Though always expected to excel, I was often told, at home and at school, that I was bossy, and admonished to refrain from showing off, hogging the limelight, and trying to impose my ideas on others. Rarely was I challenged to turn this bossiness into a strength—to learn to be a leader, to find effective ways of exciting others about things that excited me. In the church above all, the utter lack of images of female leadership made my childhood fantasies of being an apostle and a missionary romantic and

. . . . . .

unattainable. I transformed them into teenaged fantasies of marrying a minister and having six children. Then, in the secular, intellectual culture at Bryn Mawr, I eventually gave the whole package a quiet burial, deep in the recesses of my memory, where we keep our most excruciating adolescent secrets. I discovered something I did well—literary analysis—which allowed me to think and write about the things of God without embarrassing anybody, brought me showers of praise from my teachers, and did not entangle me in the sticky business of working with others and trying to remember to take a back seat.

In any case, ordination was not open to women, and it never dawned on me that within just a few years, this might change.

Since the age of nine, the center of my emotional life had been my faith. This yearning at my very core simply refused to be put down, or remain private: it cried out for expression in community and ritual, and for opportunities to belong, to serve, to teach, and to lead. I had no name for any of these desires, and (except for teaching Sunday school) no acceptable way to act on them. By now they had caused me so much frustration and embarrassment that I had a settled, unhappy sense of being weird and different. I continued to see myself as weird and different even when, by junior and senior years, I had close friends who were quite happily practicing Christians, even positively churchy—who seemed to be serious about their faith, comfortable wearing it in public, and, in a few cases, actually intending to build it into their plans for a career. But I had become so confused about the relationship of faith to the public and private self that I tried, absurdly, to push the whole business into the closet. I became both furtive and shrill about it: I had no idea how to bring it to the table as part of who I was. But, of course, it kept showing up at the table anyway.

. . . . . .

2

IT SHOWED UP most obviously in the kind of literary study I chose to do. I went to Yale to work on medieval English poetry—literature that was, often, explicitly theological and devotional. Under cover of getting a Ph.D. in English I was actually working on liturgy and theology. Then, I supposed, I would go on, find an academic job, marry Arnie, have babies, and live happily ever after. That part was less clear. I was still making decisions based on a schoolgirl's values: all I could think of was to go on doing more of what I had learned to do well—what pleased my teachers.

Still, I do not regret having majored in English. The literature itself profoundly nourished my heart, mind, and spirit. Equally important, the discipline of literary analysis taught me to respond with integrity to literary texts, to watch and analyze how people tell and hear stories; to understand how metaphor and image carry meaning and emotional power, to avoid simplistic interpretations and facile moral lessons. Much of the bad exegesis, bad preaching, and bitter controversy surrounding Scripture and liturgy in the church today arise from inappropriate responses to Scripture—misunderstandings of genre, metaphor, story, and meaning on the part of people who were never taught how to read a text.

I have left Bryn Mawr covered with honors and assured by my teachers (many of them Yale Ph.D.'s) that I will take Yale by storm. But a seachange has occurred in the Yale English Department since their time, and I find myself cast up in an alien land. I do not speak the language—semiotics, structuralism, deconstruction—and there are no introductory courses. I sit through classes peering uneasily at my classmates, trying to determine which of them are genuinely better versed in this language than I and which ones are, like me, faking it. And Arnie's warnings have been only too accurate. As the extent of the collapse in the job market becomes apparent, morale plummets and competition becomes vicious. Students fall over each other to become flatterers and sycophants of powerful faculty members. I have never been miserable in school before: I have never before despised my teachers and the entire institution.

. . . .

The Ph.D. program in English was officially a four-year course, though few candidates finished in the allotted time. My plans, such as they were, were further derailed when the senior professor in medieval English failed to return from a leave and for the next three years his place was taken by a series of visiting scholars, none of whom was available as a dissertation supervisor. Finally, a generous senior professor—a woman—agreed to supervise my dissertation, even though its topic was not in her chief area of expertise. Her motto was "Don't get it right, get it writ." I did. I finished my degree in four and a half years.

3

I AM SHARING AN APARTMENT with my sister, who is also a first-year graduate student, in art history. Arnie is living in a graduate dorm, but spending most of his evenings with us. He kisses me goodnight on the back steps of the building. He is passionate and sweet; but when is he going to ask me to marry him? I drop hints; he backs off. We go home to our families for Christmas vacation. When we come back, I have an important paper to finish, so we don't see each other right away.

Wednesday morning. I hand in my finished paper, and after class I find Arnie in the history study. I put down my notebooks. "I made it," I say.

He pushes back his chair. "Do you want to go for a walk?" I'm a little surprised; eleven o'clock in the morning is not a usual time for us to take a walk. He steers us along York Street and into the Grove Street Cemetery. It's peaceful in here; we walk for a while in silence, our arms around each other. I'm beginning to think I know what will come next. He stops and turns to me, taking both my hands.

■ ■ ■

· · · · · ·
56

Family Plot

January 1973

In the pale cold day, among gravestones
laughing I say to you, yes
Yes
a promise white-veiled, gold-ringed
serene with summer, lavender and laughter
and frozen photographs of rice and ribbons.

The body's worship in the warm dark.
A child's gold hair
blue tricycle, teddy bear, birthday candles
Easter eggs in the ardent grass
an autumn garden rain-filled with roses.

One of us, one day, a widow.

Here by the cold crosses
I bury my face in your breathing breast:
O, my love, for this life
Yes.

■ ■ ■

We were married in August, in the Bethlehem Chapel at the National Cathedral in Washington, where my brother had sung in the choir. I dived into domesticity—cooking, gardening, baking bread, sewing—found a community chorus to sing in, finished my coursework, and passed my orals. Arnie and I spent a summer in England doing research and visiting cathedrals. I contacted my old school and looked up Miss Date. She had just retired, and she squired us around the Surrey Downs and showed us the patchwork quilt, pieced from scraps of school uniforms, that her last class had made for her.

Once the course work was behind me, these were good years: a new marriage, a little basement apartment, *Piers Plowman,* and the Episcopal Church at Yale.

4

PIERS PLOWMAN IS A HUGE, untidy, gorgeous, infuriating devotional poem from the late fourteenth century, attributed to William Langland—the endlessly revised, unfinished record of one man's spiritual quest; a labyrinthine journey of the soul, portrayed as a series of visionary dreams; a tribute, finally, to the presence of Christ experienced in liturgy and community and the never-ending call to conversion of life. For me to work on it, at twenty-four and twenty-five years old, was to plunge into the labyrinth myself: to experience a kind of radical spiritual formation, to enter into the womb of Holy Church and be reborn. To work on it while also belonging to a campus chaplaincy, where daily and weekly liturgy was the heartbeat for a living fellowship of Christian friends, was a gift beyond measure.

My carrel is on the fourth floor of Sterling Library stacks. I have a shelf full of books on Piers Plowman *and medieval liturgy, and a row of ragged-looking spiral notebooks: notes from classes and reading, and the dissertation draft itself, filling three notebooks, in pencil. The notebooks are skinny, and their spirals twisted and distorted, because of my habit of tearing out a page and copying it over when it becomes too messy with corrections as I am writing it.*

The carrel's small, leaded-glass window overlooks the roofs and spires of the Yale colleges. I have stuck picture postcards around the window. At eye level, where I see it every time I look up, is a post-card of a medieval ivory plaque that my sister has sent me from her dissertation research in Germany. It shows Doubting Thomas, kneeling before the Risen Christ, with his hand thrust into Jesus' side and his head tilted sharply back to look into Jesus' face. Jesus returns Thomas's gaze. Both their faces have the timeless stillness of primitive art; they could be African wood carvings.

. . . . . .

I am working through Piers Plowman *in order, start to finish. It begins with a satirical vision of corrupt medieval society, followed by a long and tortuous pilgrimage divided into three sections with the rubrics "Dowel," "Dobet," and "Dobest" ("Do Well," "Do Better," "Do Best"). Like the poem itself, my writing winds slowly, with many delays and detours, toward its climax, the narrator's vision of Christ's descent among the dead. The soul of Christ appears as a point of light, hovering in the darkness at the gates of Hell:*

> A vois loude in that light to lucifer crieth,
> "Prynces of this place, unpynneth and unlouketh,
> For here cometh with crowne that kyng is of glorie. . . . "
> ". . . . For I that am lord of lif, love is my drynke,
> And for that drynke today I deide upon erthe.
> I faught so me thursteth yit for mannes soule sake;
> May no drynke me moiste, ne my thurste slake,
> Til the vendage falle in the vale of Josaphat,
> That I drynke right ripe must, *Resureccio mortuorum.*
> And thanne shal I come as a kyng, crouned, with Aungeles,
> And have out of helle alle mennes soules. . . . "

5

THE GREAT VIGIL OF EASTER, eleven o'clock in the darkened chapel on Yale's Old Campus. Shadowy figures, robed in ghostly white, hurry about, whispering, rustling pages, moving chairs and music stands. A thurible chain clanks and jingles; a flashlight flickers. Total darkness—time suspended.

Then: a single point of light, moving unsteadily in through the double doors with the night sky behind it; the smell of incense. The point becomes many points: all around me, the light is passed from candle to candle; faces suddenly glow out of the enveloping darkness. I am holding a lighted candle; it is bright and hot; it flickers in the unsteady drafts that blow through the chapel; it burns fast, dripping wax on my music sheets. A face hovers above the lectern in the dark: lit only by the candle she is holding, Nancy is reading the story of the seven days of creation. Singing. The ark. The Red Sea. The pillar of fire. The dry bones. Water is poured, flows over Verna's head, drips down her hair as she stands barefoot in a rubber tub on the floor. Acolytes come flocking to dry her forehead and her feet with white towels, and bundle her into an alb. The cloth looks clean, smooth, and cool, like fresh sheets, like the white robes angels wear in Flemish paintings.

We are forming a procession, singing. Shielding our candles from the night breeze, we pass through the double doors, down the steps, and, still singing, circle the Old Campus and turn back toward the chapel. Undergraduates, coming back from wherever they have been this Saturday night, stop and stare. Donald stands on the steps, the wind ruffling his hair. His voice unsteady at first, but rising, meeting the breeze and the night, he reads the Easter homily of John Chrysostom:

> Whoever is devout, and a lover of God, come, enjoy this beautiful and
> radiant Feast of Feasts! . . . Enter, all of you, into the joy of our Lord . . .
> He that was taken by Death has annihilated it! He descended into Hell,
> and took Hell captive! . . .
> Christ is risen, and Hell is overthrown! Christ is risen, and the demons
> are fallen! Christ is risen, and Life reigns! Christ is risen, and not one
> dead remains in the tombs!
> Christ is risen!
> He is risen indeed!

Donald raises a cross in his right hand:

> Christ is risen!
> He is risen indeed!
> Christ is risen!
> He is risen indeed!!!

. . . . . .

The doors are flung open. The chapel has been transformed. It is ablaze with golden light and brilliant with flowers, banners, and icons. We stream up the steps and into its glowing warmth. I am singing so hard that my voice cracks; I am no longer singing, I am roaring. Now in the full light, I look around me; eyes are bright, faces intent and rapturous. The liturgy picks up speed. Canticle piles on canticle, alleluia on alleluia. The organ, heard for the first time this night, swells into Easter hymns. Then we are all hugging each other at the peace; Arnie, in his acolyte robe, is grinning and jumping up and down. Then we are gathered, five deep, in a circle around the altar, with our hands upraised in the same gesture as the celebrant. Then the bread and the cup are passing, hand to hand. "The Body of Christ." "Amen." One or two of us drop to our knees. The remains of the loaves are replaced on the altar. The closing hymn begins: "Come ye faithful, raise the strain / Of triumphant gladness . . . ." On the second stanza, someone grabs a neighbor's hand and leads out into the open space surrounding the altar; soon a long chain of people is circling the altar, dancing, hands clasped and held high. As the hymn ends, a big table is pushed into the center of the crowd, loaded with food: the altar is cleared and more food appears on it. The party goes on and on. We learn later that some people stayed till dawn, and went up to the Divinity School for the sunrise service there.

6

IF MY DISSERTATION is ever published, I will suggest that the ivory of Doubting Thomas be the cover design. I am writing about the central role of "incarnational language" in the poem—analyzing how moments of learning and grace come through direct sensory and physical experience rather than intellectual or legalistic reasoning:

> And as alle thise wise wyes weren togideres
> In an hous al bishet and hir dore ybarred
> Crist cam in, and al closed bothe dore and yates,

. . . . . .

To Peter and to his Apostles and seide *pax vobis*;
And took Thomas by the hand and taughte hym to grope
And feele with hise fyngres his flesshliche herte.

But Piers Plowman *does not come to rest in the joy of the resurrection. The last part of the poem, ironically titled "Dobest," describes redeemed humanity descending into corruption and chaos, and the church collapsing of its own weight, attacked by Antichrist and the Seven Deadly Sins. In the final scene, the narrator, Will, embarks all over again on the pilgrimage to truth, with Conscience and Kynde (Nature) as his guides:*

"Counseille me, kynde," quod I, "what craft is best to lerne?"
"Lerne to love," quod kynde, "and leef alle othere."

"Learn to love . . . and leave all other." I am writing, at last, the final paragraphs of my dissertation.

God has acted in history; he has made possible, for anyone willing to become a pilgrim, a journey in the path of his own perfect and revealed life, by his example and with his help and accompaniment. The events of "Dobest" show that most of mankind is not willing. But there are a few who are, however imperfectly: the representatives of the awakened Conscience and the instructed Will. From our perspective . . . the shape of redemption is hard to discern among the particulars of daily tribulation and the monstrosity of sin. But it has been given, not only to Will in his dreams but to all of us in the gospel, . . . and it is actualized in this world, in every Mass and every baptism, every conversion, every repentance, every resumption of the attempt to find and become the personality that gladly gives back to God the debt of love that it owes. . . .

So the Dreamer awakes. And so the poem closes, with a challenge to

· · · · · ·

Will and to the reader: if, like Thomas, Dreamer and reader have been
in need of a special, direct, highly sensory experience of God, God has
given it. If even the gospel and the sacramental rhetoric of Holy Church
have been perceived as mere precept and disputation, mere logic and law,
now the whole visionary experience of the poem has provided the
incarnation to follow and transcend it—the love to fulfill law, the
"Dobet" to give life to the thin and theoretical "Dowel" we had known.
God has intervened; now it is time to respond and be converted.

*Arnie and I are finishing our dissertations for the same deadline; they are due in ten days. I have just
started a nine-to-five job at the Yale Library to bring in some income so that he can devote full time to
the job search. He still wants to be a scholar. I know now that I do not, though I don't know what I
do want. We are paying a professional typist to do his dissertation. To save money, I am doing mine
myself, on a manual typewriter. I'm a fast, neat typist, but I am realizing with mounting panic that I
have not allowed enough time to type 250 pages of text, with quotations in Middle English, footnotes
at the bottom of the page, and a long bibliography. I am forced to work late into the night, night after
night, and to cut corners on proofreading.*

*In the English department, dissertation readers are chosen by the faculty and do not include the
student's advisor. My readers are a junior professor, an adjunct, and one tenured professor. The adjunct's
comments are enthusiastic, the junior professor's noncommittal. The senior faculty member devotes most
of his report to enumerating the several dozen typing errors he has found in the manuscript.*

. . . . . .

PART SIX

'Twas grace that taught my heart to fear,
and grace my fears relieved;
how precious did that grace appear
the hour I first believed!

1

"GOD HAS INTERVENED; now it is time to respond and be converted."

Who was I talking to—who was I writing for? My advisor and readers' committee were the only audience I was likely ever to have for the two years' worth of work that had carried me into the heart of Scripture, liturgy, and my own yearning for God. There was no prospect of my dissertation being published if I did not go on with an academic career; but I had deliberately distanced myself from cutting-edge literary theory and, more importantly, I had learned that my own mind is creative and synthetic rather than scholarly or speculative. I would have been glad to teach—especially to teach *Piers Plowman*—if I could have taught it for what I believed it to be: a poem about faith, which, as one of its commentators remarked, "fastens on an experience of conversion, with the aim of effecting another." There was, in any case, virtually no chance of both Arnie and myself finding academic jobs in the same geographic area. We chose to concentrate on finding just one, for him. Then I would decide what came next for me.

■ ■ ■

My job is with the Historical Sound Recordings collection at the Yale Library. It's a pleasant place to work, though the pay is woefully low. The thousands of early 78 rpm records are filed by their serial numbers and hand-indexed into a card catalog. After the disorientation of the early weeks, I begin to get confident. I can do this; if I work hard I can get really good at it. Then it dawns on me: I have no interest in getting really good at it. I'll do it well, of course. But it's just a job.

■ ■ ■

The two chaplains who gave the Episcopal Church at Yale its distinctive character have moved on. We will be calling a new chaplain in February. Many of the vestments and all of the icons belonged to the former chaplains, and there is no budget to replace them. Several of us determine to create new ones. I am designing them and supervising the informal guild of embroiderers and stitchers that gathers to help. There will be three huge banners, based on the tympanum at Moissac. The central banner will show Christ in glory, framed in a mandala, with the words, "Behold I make all things new." The other two show the four winged Living Creatures of the Apocalypse. Kneeling on the kitchen floor, transferring my enlarged designs to tissue paper, I am completely happy and absorbed in my work. This is a crazy project; there is no way we can complete it in time for Easter. But we do. The majestic figure of Jesus hovers amid ripples of turquoise, red, and orange on a gold ground. His face is stern but gracious. I am filled with elation. Maybe I should design banners for a living.

■ ■ ■

A college friend calls me up with an idea. Would I like to collaborate on a prayer book for children? Children are now receiving communion at six or seven or even younger, instead of having to wait till confirmation; but there does not seem to exist a children's version of the new prayer book, to help them take part in the service. She would write the text, and I'd do the illustrations.

We mail drafts and sample pages back and forth to each other and to several church-related publishers. We send some samples to Madeleine L'Engle, who has done a retreat for ECY, and she is enthusiastic. No publisher, however, is interested. Another dead end.

. . . . . .

2

I AM AT ST. PAUL'S CHURCH, for the installation of their new rector. St. Paul's is where we go during the summers and other times when the Episcopal Church at Yale, along with the rest of Yale, goes dormant. Several of us ECY types have been pressed into service today to augment the parish choir. St. Paul's was once a flagship parish in New Haven but has fallen on hard times. Today, the church is crowded with guests, well-wishers, and friends, but on a normal Sunday the congregation—a remnant after many years of conflict and crisis—is thinly scattered in the colossal Victorian nave. The crimson carpet is frayed, the paint dingy. The parish has a long history of social outreach and is now spending down its endowment to pay for two clergy—the new rector and a young black assistant—in an effort to regain ground and continue its neighborhood ministries with children and youth.

The new rector is a prophetic preacher and political activist who has written a book on urban ministry. He seems to turn up everywhere, and remembers everyone's name. I run into him at a party and find myself telling war stories about teaching Sunday school at St. Mary's. The Episcopal Church, I hear myself saying, has become criminally negligent about Christian education and children in general. I am surprised at my own vehemence: for the last four years I have been happily immersed in the campus chaplaincy, where there is, of course, no Sunday school. Now the rector of St. Paul's is challenging me to put my money where my mouth is: his parish needs Sunday school teachers; would I be interested? I think about it for a second. Yes, I would.

Sunday school meets in the undercroft, which was built a decade ago, just before the church began its steep decline. The room has seen heavy use by the parish's after-school and summer programs with neighborhood children. It has scuffed beige walls, grey industrial carpeting, a sprayed asbestos ceiling, and six small bays around the perimeter, partitioned off as classrooms using accordion doors. The doors have come out of their tracks and are stuck in various stages of open and closed. The asbestos ceiling is coming loose; powdery grey threads hang in cascades from the ceiling. The cabinets are a jumble of dusty supplies and discarded curriculum materials.

. . . . . .

Thanks to the neighborhood ministry, the parish has a large Sunday school for such a small congregation. The fifth and sixth graders in my class are mostly black. Many of them walk to church from the immediate neighborhood; their parents are nowhere in evidence. The kids are sweet to me; they help me remember their names, and show me where to find the supplies. In church for communion, they are goofy and distractible. Mark, one of the fifth graders, blows bubble gum at the communion rail. I play the heavy with him, and he teases me about it. I can afford to be attentive to the kids here in the morning. At five o'clock Sunday afternoon, I'll be in Dwight Chapel for the Sunday liturgy with ECY.

In March, the rector announces that the bishop will be coming for confirmation in May, and the sixth graders in the class will be confirmed, so could I please prepare them? I am stunned: if I had known this earlier, I would have built the whole year around it. And what of the fifth graders? Mark, in particular, is much more earnest about the church than most of the sixth graders; he would be a far more apt candidate than his big brother, Keith, who is utterly blasé about the whole business. But I have no say in the question, so I get down to business and create a workbook from the catechism at the back of the new Book of Common Prayer. The kids labor slowly through it, week by week. I think of them constantly. I want so much for them to feel the same sense of joy and privilege about their confirmation as I did. I have no idea what they are thinking. I pray for them when Arnie and I sit together after supper for our evening prayers: Darrell, Patricia, Suzy, Keith, Jenny, the sixth graders; Mark and Carrie, who are in fifth grade and will not be confirmed. I realize I am giving far more attention and thought to these kids than I ever gave to the Yale undergraduates in my section of the Shakespeare course when I was a teaching assistant several years ago.

Confirmation day. As I arrive for the service, there is a traffic jam in the doorway. Mark is sobbing in the arms of the assistant priest. "It's not fair, it's not fair," he gasps, his shoulders shaking. "Keith always gets to do everything first. I want to be confirmed too! I'm just as ready as he is." "It's OK, man," the assistant keeps saying, over and over. "It'll be your turn next year."

. . . . . .

3

ARNIE IS TIRED AND TENSE, stretched thin by the competing demands of several part-time jobs at various branches of the State University system, rewriting his dissertation for publication, and applying for the handful of openings in his field of study. We can't afford a car, so his commuting, which includes teaching an evening class some forty miles away, is insanely complicated. We agonize over whether he should apply for a one-year temporary opening at the University of New Mexico. What would we do after that one year? We'd be stuck out there, where we don't know anybody. He has begun to consider prep schools as well as colleges. We go together to several interviews, but nothing pans out. Then there are no more local teaching jobs; now Arnie is working as a security guard. He is talking about going to law school. But how would we pay for it? And suppose the market collapsed there too? Recent Ph.D.'s are jumping to law school in droves. I try to be supportive, but I am getting impatient. We have been married four years, and I am starting to want a baby.

The three-room basement apartment that was cozy when we were students now feels small and dingy. We snap at each other. We know we have to get through this together; we pray together; we talk to the chaplain, but everything seems forced and unreal. The liturgy, for the first time in years, is no longer a comfort. There is tension there too—the members are divided over changes the new chaplain has introduced. I try to go directly to God. I read the Bible; texts that once challenged and thrilled me now seem filled with terror; texts that were full of promise now seem hollow and false. I don't want to be a hero and a martyr. I want Arnie to get a job so we can have a baby. I'm angry with God. What more innocent goal can anyone have, I ask God through clenched teeth as I bicycle furiously to work, than to do what they love and have trained for, and to establish a Christian family? What are you waiting for?

. . . . . .

4

TWICE A YEAR, ECY arranges a retreat. I have never gone to one; I don't think of myself as one of the spiritual adepts, and the idea of silence is scary. But in desperation I sign up for the November retreat on "Prayer," led by an English monk. It will be held at Holy Cross Monastery in the Hudson Valley.

The car I am in is driven by an undergraduate. We get lost on the way and arrive late. The others have been worrying about us. Father G. is already sitting with the group, explaining the rules for the retreat. He has asked for all of our names so that he can pray for us. I ask him if it is permitted for me to work on the embroidery I am doing for the vestment project. No, he tells me; we are here to empty our minds, hands and hearts for God to enter. I can feel the resistance rising up inside myself: I'm not sure I want God to enter. I'm not on good terms with God right now. Maybe I shouldn't have come.

Matins . . . breakfast (silent) . . . meditation with Father G. . . . silence . . . eucharist. Meals and liturgy, meditations and silence follow each other in a steady, gently pulsing rhythm all through the day. I look around me in the chapel during one of the silences. There are my friends, scattered through the rows of chairs. The chapel is filled with their breathing, inaudible but palpably present. As I sit, erect and still, the whole chapel becomes as one body, enclosing all of us in its breathing core. I close my eyes. I am alone, but not lonely. I open my eyes and my gaze falls on the crucifix. He is here, too.

The silence has become like an embrace; the silence has become like water, searching out the chinks in my armor, trickling through, dampening me, finally soaking me, immersing me. The silence sees me and I have nothing to hide. There is no hurry; there is nothing to be impatient for; there is nothing to want. The silent, waiting God does not owe me anything, and will give me whatever he chooses; I am to open my hands to receive it, and all will be well. I have entered so deeply into the silence that on Sunday morning, when the organist begins to practice the morning's hymns during our last meditation, I feel it as a rude intrusion, even though he is playing "At the Name of Jesus," one of my very favorites.

I come home, and peace comes with me. "You've changed," says Arnie, and I try to explain to him what is different, and help him find it, too. I suggest that he spend a morning at home, in silence. He

. . . . . .

tries it, and it helps, some. And he has made a decision: he will not hold out any longer for an acade-mic job, and he will not go back to school.

In March, the State of Connecticut offered Arnie a career traineeship as a research ana-lyst. By the time he started the job in April, I was pregnant. We moved to a larger apartment in August; Grace was born in early December.

5

LEARNING OF the pregnancy just after Easter, in the midst of a spiritual reawakening, I antic-ipated a wondrous journey of praise and oneness with God the creator of all life. I started a journal:

> I went for a walk on Saturday full of the sense of the bursting of new life—almost in tears with the strength of it. All life is a type of the Resurrection—it is a defiance of the principle of entropy. Matter has-tens to organize itself and to pull other matter into this organization: how unnatural! how miraculous!

Within only a few weeks, however, I was noting that my new state had "thrown a monkey wrench into my spiritual life"—I was reaching for the rapidly growing stack of books on pregnancy instead of for the Bible. I felt powerless to resist this change. Having just begun to open my arms, to lift my face, towards God, I was now watching myself curl up to sur-round and embrace the child within me, and somehow this also meant turning my back to the mysterious Presence who had sought and found me in the silence at the retreat. I felt myself pulled in two directions: I felt I simply could not go both ways at once.

I was still eager, even passionate, to lead and to teach. I developed a small summer Bible study for several middle-school children from St. Paul's, brought them to the Yale campus, and fed them supper once a week. They giggled at my belly, and one week I found myself teaching them basic sex education. I was at home in two churches; I was busy and happy. But the complete freedom, love, and trust I had found, the unmediated union with the Holy One—that was gone.

"LO CHILDREN, and the fruit of the womb, are an heritage and gift that cometh of the Lord," read the birth announcements, hand-printed from a linoleum block, which we sent out in place of Christmas cards. *"Born to Arnold and Gretchen Pritchard: a daughter, Grace Martha."* It was an easy pregnancy—on the day I went into labor, I was still riding my bicycle around town, doing Christmas shopping—but labor was long and complicated; I developed a high fever and the baby and I both needed antibiotics. It was nothing to worry about, except that I knew enough to be acutely aware that in the days before modern medicine we would probably both have died.

"The Lord giveth, and the Lord taketh away": *I have become terrified of the huge, hostile emptiness beyond the safe warm circle of my own arms. I wake up in tears from dreams that the baby is lost, that the baby is dead. "Darling, darling, darling," I am sobbing, "I loved you so much." But there she still is, right next to our bed, asleep in the cradle that Arnie's father has made for us. I reach down and touch her warm, firm little back. I stare hungrily at her. She is mine and yet not mine, and I cannot assure myself that she will always be safe.*

She was born during exam week at Yale. Student friends from ECY, who had eagerly offered to visit and help out, called one after another to explain that they just couldn't make it; then they left town for Christmas. After Christmas, my mother, visiting us from Washington, confirmed my growing suspicion that the baby had a congenital hip dislocation, which my sister and I had also had. The pediatrician said she was fine; I had to insist on a consultation with the orthopedist, who spotted the problem immediately. At this early stage it was easy to treat, but the experience further deepened my sense of vulnerability. Then in February the divisions that had been simmering within the chaplaincy exploded. The weekly prayer group split into two factions, and there was a huge, ugly blowup. People stopped speaking to each other; rumors and allegations flew back and forth by phone; several members left the congregation entirely. Civility was restored within a few weeks, but lasting damage had been done.

Home alone with the baby—her legs carefully held in the correct position by foam-lined overalls my mother had sewn for her—I felt I had lost my entire support network, the circle of Christian friends we had been counting on to surround us and our child with love. When the rector of St. Paul's called to ask if I would be interested in a part-time job as the Sunday school director ("and bring the baby"), I accepted at once.

Grace was baptized at the Easter Vigil at ECY, in an earthenware font that we had commissioned from a local craftsman as a thank offering, using part of Arnie's small legacy from his grandmother, after whom Grace was named. Arnie's mother stood proxy for Miss Date as one of her godmothers. Once she was baptized, I began to feel a little safer. The school year was almost over. The chaplain took us aside. "It's time for you to move on," he said. "You're ten years older than the freshmen; you have a child; you're no longer affiliated with Yale; you have a job at St. Paul's. That should be your parish." He was right, of course. And we should have seen it for ourselves. But we never were any good at letting go.

. . . . . .

PART SEVEN

· · · · ·

Furrows, be glad. Though earth is bare,
one more seed is planted there:
give up your strength the seed to nourish
that in course the flow'r may flourish.
   People, look East, and sing today:
   Love the Rose is on the way.

1

I SPENT MY FIRST SIX MONTHS as a staff member at St. Paul's getting to know the parish and cleaning up the unbelievable mess in the undercroft. I came to work one day a week, and nursed the baby during the staff meeting; she would fall asleep, and I would leave her on the couch in the rector's office. When she woke up, he would play with her and then bring her downstairs, where I had spread a receiving blanket on the grubby carpeting that was thick with asbestos dust. Innocent of the enormity of the task, I organized a painting party to freshen up the undercroft in ice-cream parlor colors. Dozens of people turned out, and we almost got the job done. A friend of mine finished it up, for pay. No sooner was the undercroft done than Arnie, who had been doing some research, confronted the vestry about the asbestos. It took an ad hoc committee (chaired by Arnie), a loan from the diocese, and two years, but the asbestos was removed. Sunday school moved to the parish hall—as it turned out, a much better space. It never returned to the basement. And Arnie and I are still haunted by the image of baby Grace, lying on her tummy with her nose in the grey carpet.

October. We have met with a consultant and chosen the latest curriculum, developed by the Diocese of Colorado. The principle behind it is great—the same Scriptures that are read in the congregation should form the basis of the Sunday school lesson. But the developers have not provided any visual

· · · · ·

materials for the children. As the day's lesson is read aloud, their eyes glaze over. I am sitting in the parish office, going through back issues of an Episcopal Church education resource called Aware. *There is an article by John Conbere describing cartoons he drew for his church school kids at St. Thomas's in Hanover, New Hampshire. Now there's an idea, I think. I work up the week's readings as crude cartoons, and decide they need a name.* The Sunday Comics—*no,* The Sunday Paper. *I mail a copy to each kid, in advance of Sunday morning. Everybody loves it. Now I'm committed; I have to do it every week.*

December: Grace's first birthday. She is little and dainty, with a cloud of almost white curls. She is just learning to walk; she staggers all around our little apartment clutching her grandfather's finger while he prances along beside her, laughing his big laugh. I am taking pictures. In the background of the photographs, the table is strewn with pastel taffeta in three colors, and rolls of milliner's buckram. Angel costumes for the Christmas pageant.

There has been no Christmas pageant at St. Paul's for more than fifteen years. The parish families have told me that a Christmas pageant is their next priority after choosing a curriculum and cleaning up the space. I have not needed much persuading. This is something I know how to do. I type up a script, lifting some of the lines directly from the plays my sister and brother and I used to put on as children:

Joseph: Look, Mary, I see the lights of David's city.
Mary: Thanks be to God. I can scarcely go another step.

The rehearsals are harder than I anticipated; the kids, after all, can't read my mind; I have to figure out how to explain to them what I am expecting. Parents, more experienced with primary-aged children than I am, tactfully help out. There are two costume-sewing marathons and we rescue some ancient costumes from the church cellar, including a spectacular donkey head. The pageant is a great success; I am basking in the gratitude and admiration of the children's parents.

. . . . . .

Next, I tackle Holy Week. Nobody who has experienced Holy Week at ECY can fail to realize that Easter, not Christmas, is the pinnacle of the church's year: I want the kids to begin to grasp this. I want to raise the parish's consciousness, too. With the Christian Nurture Committee, I plan a "one-day Bible camp" on the eve of Palm Sunday, to introduce the children to as many as possible of the images and themes of the season. Turnout is one hundred percent, except for one child who is "on punishment"—grounded. We are on a roll.

2

SHORTLY AFTER I JOINED THE STAFF of St. Paul's, the rector was elected bishop and left in a blaze of glory. The assistant's position had been cut for budgetary reasons. After an easy, one-year interim, a new rector was called: he was young, energetic, engaging, extroverted; a gifted preacher, with unkempt hair and a beard. He had two small children; his little daughter became Grace's playmate. The parish began attracting young, educated, white families. Sunday school and adult education grew by leaps and bounds.

Response to my cartoons has been so favorable that I have been persuaded to try distributing them beyond the parish. I have written an article for Aware, *and the creators of the Colorado curriculum have inserted a leaflet describing* The Sunday Paper *in their fall mailing. The phone has been ringing off the hook. I find myself developing a small business by the seat of my pants. I am struggling with billing, record keeping, and mailing list management with only a small desk, a manual typewriter, and some card file boxes. Copies of the first batch of fall issues, which we failed to have the printer collate for us, are spread out all over the living room floor. Grace, twenty months old, picks her way gingerly around the mess, amid constant warnings: "No, no! Don't touch Mommy's work!" Late on a sweaty August night, we have bundled the last of the addressed envelopes and stuffed them in boxes to take to the post office. I have photographed the whole process, ending with Arnie, damp and hollow-eyed, sitting on the floor with the completed boxes. When the photographs are developed, I show them to*

Grace. *"What's that?"* I ask, expecting her to say, *"Mommy's work."* *"No no!!"* she says, wagging her finger. *"No no no!"*

The Sunday Paper grew. I hired a friend as part-time helper to manage the record-keeping and stuff the envelopes. Eight months later, I did a direct-mail ad to every Episcopal parish. The business tripled overnight. It was an ideal situation: I had a flexible part-time job that got me out of the house, and the rest of the time I was working at home and could be with my child. I was doing work I believed in and did well, and I was making money.

St. Paul's grew. When the kids seemed bored with the same Christmas pageant script two years in a row, I wrote a new one, based on medieval mystery plays. "Palm Saturday" became an institution, later joined by "All Saints' Saturday." The rector's casual, somewhat corny style, his political liberalism, his highly personal preaching, and the parish's reputation for inclusiveness, filled the pews with people who had written off the whole idea of church and now felt that here, and here alone, was the Spirit alive. The Worship and Music Committee began to deepen and enrich the parish's liturgical life, with special attention to Holy Week and the Easter Vigil. I was learning, doing new things, and having fun. I even taught an adult education class on *Piers Plowman.*

Our family grew. Grace started nursery school; I was pregnant with our second child. This pregnancy was not so easy. I was nauseated; I kept getting sinus infections and bronchitis; coughing day and night, I twice cracked a rib and spent days doubled over in pain. Through it all, I was trying to keep up with a three-year-old and get ahead on my work in order to have time with the new baby. We were bursting the walls of our four-room apartment. With the new-found financial security from *The Sunday Paper,* we bought a small two-family house. Suddenly we were not only homeowners but landlords. Margaret was born at dawn on May Day; we brought her home to the apartment and spent the next two months commuting between there and the new house, packing, cleaning, spackling, painting, unpacking, organizing. We had a housewarming party when she was baptized (with five other babies) on All Saints' Day.

We were busier than we had ever been in our lives. I quit the community chorus where I had been singing since graduate school; there was no time. I quit sewing and baking bread. We had long ago severed our connection with ECY, so there were no more Sunday afternoon liturgies to supply me with the transcendence that was lacking at St. Paul's, and the preaching I was missing by being in Sunday school. Like the parish, I was spending down my endowment.

3

GRACE WAS NEVER SICK in her life till she was over a year old, but this baby is different. With a big sister in nursery school, she catches every germ that goes around. Colds, diarrhea, ear infections. Antibiotics, vomiting, another cold. She wakes up in the mornings with her eyes, nose, and mouth crusted with green mucus. She has been eating solid food, but she loses her appetite for days on end; she gags on the mucus and throws up. She is still nursing five or six times a day, so we are casual about her eating: we are busy; we are sick much of the time ourselves; Arnie has pneumonia for three weeks in November; I have repeated bouts of tonsillitis. We're no longer first-time parents, keeping track of everything the baby does. It isn't till her twelve-month checkup that we discover she has gained only five ounces in the last three months. They try to test her for food allergies, but now she has turned against all solid food. She is actually losing weight. We are told to force-feed her; if she does not begin to gain, she will be hospitalized for failure to thrive.

We are trying to force-feed her. It takes two of us. Arnie holds her head so she cannot turn away, while I pry her mouth open and push in the spoon. It is a disaster: she has learned not only to spit out the food but to vomit deliberately. She wants to nurse day and night. I am not equal to this: I am tired and worried and on antibiotics myself. The doctors order me to wean her, to put her on soy for-

mula. She refuses the bottle, scrabbling at my shirt. I rock her and rock her. We are both in tears. Finally, she accepts a bottle from Arnie, if the soy formula is spiked with concentrated apple juice. This becomes her only food for almost a year. She gains weight and becomes an adorable, cuddly toddler, bursting with personality. But she has learned to use her ability to vomit as a weapon, to get us into her room when she does not want to go to sleep.

The one solid food she does not refuse is the eucharist.

■ ■ ■

I am exhausted; I am overwhelmed. At church, I am just going through the motions. I'm nearly always angry, at how much drudgery the job involves, and how, after everything I have done, the children don't seem to learn anything; the parents are more committed to Sunday morning soccer than to church; and the building is always filthy and disorderly. I exhort, I nag, I scold; nothing makes any difference. The rector teases me and calls me passive-aggressive. At home, I have to draw an issue of The Sunday Paper each week, and stay eight weeks ahead of dateline. It is an endless treadmill.

Margaret is in the playpen; maybe she'll let me get some work done before we have to go pick up Grace from nursery school. The phone rings; it's a customer with a question. If they had read the order form carefully, they wouldn't have had to bother me. Why are so many church people such jerks? I go back to my work. I am drawing Jesus, healing the sick. He is a simple figure, easy to draw. Nearly always, he is smiling. I can make him do whatever I want. I can make him smile or frown; sit, stand, reach out and touch other people or get up and walk away. The whole business is making me uneasy—slightly sick to my stomach. Maybe this is why the Ten Commandments forbid graven images.

■ ■ ■

I am working on a book, to be called Alleluia! Amen. This is a reincarnation of the Children's prayer book concept of six years ago. My hunch is that I no longer need a publisher: if I redesign the *book along the lines of* The Sunday Paper, *I can bring it out under my own imprint. I bet it will sell. Maybe it will put the kids through college. Something will have to. It is a daunting project. I will have to find more time, somehow.*

My mother is throwing a big party in Washington for my father's seventieth birthday. I'm too busy, I tell her. I just can't make it.

My mother-in-law is decorated by the Israeli government for her heroism in sheltering Jews during World War II, when she was a young social worker in Amsterdam. The ceremony is at the Israeli consulate in Boston. I'm too busy, I tell her. I just can't make it.

"Lerne to love," quod Kynde, "and leef alle othere."

Something is wrong.

4

I TOLD THE RECTOR that I had reached the end of my rope and something had to go; it was time for me to quit the job of Christian education coordinator. He persuaded me to take a year's sabbatical, instead, and to keep coming to staff meetings to stay in touch.

I began keeping a journal again.

> At the moment the biggest problems are spiritual: I'm scared of God—
> what he wants out of me (everything—he's never satisfied, he'll never
> leave me alone to decide for myself what I want—he'll never say,
> "Good—you've finished that job") and what he might do to me (espe-
> cially to my kids . . . and what he is doing and has done to millions of
> others). . . . The Christianity I had at ECY before I became a parent
> now seems incredibly naïve, academic, and provincial; but what St. Paul's
> has to offer instead of it seems totally unaddressed to my condition.

What St. Paul's had to offer was a study group I rudely referred to as the "Henri Nouwen fan club," and a rector who had begun obsessing on nuclear war. "Do not worry," was Nouwen's theme in a book on the Sermon on the Mount that we were studying. Examples from the Desert Fathers exhorted us to inner peace and trust in God. To me, the entire business seemed addressed only to solitary adepts with nothing more urgent to concern them than the finer points of their own spiritual progress. Nouwen's mild admonitions on the futility of worry struck me as facile, celibate dismissal of the real anguish of parents, children, and the poor. I was the only parent in the group, and felt completely unheard and ununderstood by the other members. Wrestling with the elemental fierceness of my love for my children, and a kind of nameless terror in sympathy with the sufferings of others (and a free-floating anxiety about nuclear and ecological catastrophe, abetted by the rector's concerns), I found myself helplessly enraged: *if this is spirituality, it has nothing to say to me; it strains at a gnat and swallows a camel.*

And when I turned to the gospels themselves, especially the Sermon on the Mount, I found an invitation not to peace and trust but to a degree of self-abandonment that filled me with terror and dismay, and then with defensive outrage. *How can anybody with children be expected to take these texts seriously? And yet many have been driven to—by war, by poverty, by conscience, perhaps even by love. Is any of this stuff addressed to me? I don't know. I don't want to know.* Meanwhile the rector, in an effort to stir the congregation to activism, was painting ever more graphic scenarios of nuclear holocaust in the pulpit and the parish newsletter. I felt torn apart by what I perceived as condemnation, equally vehement, from two equal and opposite voices, the study group's and the rector's.

> They condemn me for worrying; he implicitly condemns me for not
> worrying! . . . and God is saying *nothing*, but daily receding and seeming

· · · · · ·

less and less real and less and less attractive. . . . In one way or another, ever since Grace was born, I have been saying to God, "Promise me you won't touch my babies, and show me what you want, and I'll do it— *only then promise that you absolutely won't touch my babies. . . .*"

I went on another retreat and came back even more alienated and confused than before. The answer, this time, would be found not in solitude, but in community.

5

"WHAT A RELIEF IT IS, to be working with a product rather than with people," somebody wrote in the Bryn Mawr *Alumnae Bulletin* after a midlife career change. On leave from the Sunday school job at St. Paul's, I knew exactly what she meant. I was no longer responsible for "program"—for motivating people and keeping them happy, for worrying about whether I was being bossy and coming on too strong—and I no longer had to stand up on Sundays in front of the children and exhort them to a trust and enthusiasm I did not feel. I could relax a little. I worked on the communion book; I puttered away at organizing the parish library; I read; I worked in my garden; I lay fallow and tried to pray. Nothing happened; God was still silent, inscrutable, severe, or absent. But at least nobody was *watching* me.

My friend Sherry filled in for me at St. Paul's. Sherry is, by her own description, a "take-charge person." She pestered the vestry to remodel part of the parish hall, creating several much-needed classrooms; she shook up the Christmas pageant: instead of a nativity play performed by the children in place of the sermon, she turned the whole liturgy on the Fourth Sunday of Advent into a celebration—a miscellany of dramatized Scripture readings, carols, and instrumental music, performed by kids, adults, and teens together. A teenaged dancer, in the role of the star of Bethlehem, tossed handfuls of glitter at Mary and the shepherds. And Sherry was the one who pushed me, while I had the time, to take on a project we had both dreamed of for several years: a parish production of *The Man Born to Be King*, Dorothy Sayers's series of radio plays on the life of Christ.

There are twelve plays. I have loved them since I first discovered Dorothy Sayers, right after college. They are tough, realistic drama, written, according to Sayers, "not to instruct but to show forth; not to point to a moral but to tell a story." We will do the first one, about the Three Kings, at a parish party on Epiphany, and the second, on Jesus' baptism, at the ten-thirty service on the following Sunday. I have edited the scripts, assembled a cast, assigned roles, and worked out a seating plan for the performers so that the dialogue flows naturally—a challenge, since most participants are playing several different parts.

This is the first time I have worked directly with adults. What will they think of me? Why are they doing this—because I asked them and they didn't want to say no, or because they really want to do it? I am thirty-three years old, and I still approach the vast majority of adults with the nine-year-old's settled conviction that grownups never understand what you think is really important.

The plays went well. They were fun—especially the sound effects. People were impressed, and deeply moved. We were surprised at ourselves: *"Hey, we are good!"* We decided to keep going. Every couple of months, except during the summer, a play replaced the sermon at the Sunday morning service. The dozen of us who began the project eventually formed the core of a little guild of *Man Born to Be King* players. I was no longer just the pushy Sunday school director. I was a leader, and adults in the parish had become my friends.

· · · · · ·

6

I HAVE FINISHED Alleluia! Amen, *and it's selling faster than I can fill orders. And I'm back at work, with a new job title I have chosen for myself: Minister of Christian Nurture. I'm planning the Christmas pageant. Building on Sherry's innovations, I have planned a dramatized festival of lessons and carols that will involve adults and children together and comprise the entire Sunday morning liturgy. It will begin with Adam and Eve and end with a reading from Revelation. Instead of the star of Bethlehem tossing glitter, we will have the Angel of the Lord. At the offertory, adults and children will join hands and dance around the altar.*

Nine lessons, nine carols; a tree at the center which begins as the tree of knowledge and becomes the tree of Jesse, then the Christmas tree, then the cross, and finally the tree of life. The script writes itself. I am in awe of what I have done. This is liturgy: *profound, stirring, full of images and metaphors that call forth meaning from each other. We have only three rehearsals. Though there are no lines to memorize, the scale of the production is daunting: this is not a Sunday school pageant. Children are nervous, adults skeptical; there is muttering and a rising sense of panic. I am the only one who sees the whole. The night before the last rehearsal I am trying vainly to relax. "It's a fabulous script, it just has to work," I say to Arnie. "It'll work," he says. But I lie in the darkness, rigid and terrified: I have taken on too much.*

Sunday morning: we have crammed in a last rehearsal before the service begins. This is it: the shofar sounds, the lights come up. Adam and Eve, played by seventh graders, stand in skintight leotards flanking the tree. They pluck the fruit; the Angel of the Lord, in eucharistic vestments, stands sternly before them and banishes them with a sweep of his hand to the back of the church. All the children come out from the choir stalls and crouch around the tree, wearing animal masks; the angel fills the tree with doves—the Peaceable Kingdom. Adam and Eve return and are robed and crowned; the angel hangs a star in the tree. Robbie (Adam) catches my eye and grins, "I didn't know it would go this fast!" Mary, suspecting nothing, is sweeping the floor; the angel bursts upon her and showers her with glitter;

the congregation gasps. Joseph, animals, angels, shepherds: everyone has glitter in their hair. Passing the peace: hugs, laughter, congratulations, "Is it over?"— "No, we still have to do the dance!"

> Sing O my love, O my love, my love, my love:
> This have I done for my true love.

The bread and the cup have passed around the circle of children; they have re-formed the manger tableau and sung their carols. We are streaming down the chancel steps, singing "Go, tell it on the mountain," clustering at the back of the church. Panic strikes me: does Lee, the organist, remember that there is one more reading before the postlude? I dash upstairs to the organ loft. Lee finishes the hymn with a flourish and swivels round on his bench. Far away, on the chancel steps, Marsden—the Angel of the Lord— is standing alone beside the tree.

> I am the Alpha and the Omega, the first and the last, the beginning and
> the end. Blessed are those who wash their robes, that they may have the
> right to the tree of life, and that they may enter the city by the gates. . . .
> The Spirit and the Bride say, "Come." . . . He who testifies to these
> things says, "Surely I am coming soon—"

"Amen! Come, Lord Jesus!" comes the response—and with a magnificent flourish, Marsden flings a shower of glitter over the congregation, and the church explodes with applause. This was not in the script. Lee swivels back around and launches into the postlude. Leaning over the balcony railing, I am shaking with sobs.

"It was The Sunday Paper *brought to life," one of the parents tells me later.*

. . . . . .

THE MAN BORN TO BE KING extended over fifteen months. Over a year after we had begun, four months after the new Christmas pageant, the four Passion plays were mounted as a Lenten program, one every Wednesday night, and the series concluded with the Easter play on the Sunday after Easter. The Passion sequence became, for us and for the audience (which grew from week to week), an immersion experience that left us utterly spent. It was not until Easter that I realized how *The Man Born to Be King* had become liturgy for us. While Holy Week had regathered and lifted up the plays, carrying us into a profound and over-whelming anamnesis that was almost more than we could bear, Easter left us curiously unconsummated, wondering what had not quite clicked. Then we gathered on Low Sunday to do the final play.

Peter: See there, where the body lay . . . The grave-bands, criss-crossed and wound together from breast to foot. . . . Who can have arranged them like that—and in Heaven's name, why?

John: Nobody!—nobody!— . . . Can't you see?—They have never been unwound. . . . Look! here is a bundle of myrrh still fast among the folds.

Peter: Never unwound?—You are mad! How could the body have passed—?

John: Risen and gone! Risen and gone!—O Jesus! my friend and my living Lord!

Lee, our choir director, a deeply devout man then in his sixties, played the part of John. Deeply devout—but none of us had ever before heard from his lips an affirmation of faith that shook the church to its rafters.

· · · · · ·

Arnie, as Cleophas, breathless and excited: "So we ran back all the way to Jerusalem to tell you . . . It's true, you see, after all!" . . . Harriet, playing James, welcoming the risen Lord with the utmost simplicity: "Come and sit down, won't you?"

And I gave myself the part of Mary Magdalene.

Each of us, in character, was able to say what we had never said before, to God and to each other; and for each of us, it was exactly what we needed to say. The rector, half-embarrassed, told me the next day that he had had to fight back the impulse, after the service, to fall on his knees before Curtis, who had played Jesus for almost the entire series.

Three days later: I have been singing, all week, a folk carol I heard on the radio last Friday, before the play.

>Down came an angel,
>Down came an angel
>Down came an angel,
>And rolled the stone away.
>
>Mary, she came weeping . . .
>Her precious Lord to seek.
>
>What's the matter, Mary? . . .
>They stole my Lord away.

I am climbing the stone steps behind the chapel at the Yale Divinity School, on my way to the library to return a book. The cherry trees flanking the steps are in full, glorious bloom, their branches tossing under a polished blue sky. Halfway up the steps, I stop. Something is there, a clear wall, a presence, almost palpable; it touches me, it presses upon me; I can barely breathe. I push through it, and I am changed. Spring has come; the whole world is big with God; every leaf, every blossom, every person in the quadrangle is radiant with eternal meaning.

. . . . . .

God is good; I do not have to know what that means.
God is Lord; I do not have to know what that means.
God suffers with us, and that is enough.

Go and tell your brethren,
Go and tell your brethren,
Go and tell your brethren,
That Christ is risen today.

"I must preach Christ."

Suddenly, I am outside myself, looking at myself. I am standing on a stage, with my back to the audience, tossing back over my shoulder, one after another, wrapped packages that fall into people's laps. The people open them. "Oh! Just what I wanted! A picture of God."

. . . . . .

PART EIGHT

Now with gladness, now with courage,
    bear the burden on thee laid,
that hereafter these thy labors
    may with endless gifts be paid,
and in everlasting glory
    thou with brightness be arrayed.

1

WOE UNTO ME if I proclaim not the gospel! Ideas, images, plans spill out of me and overflow. I begin a book on baptism to go with Alleluia! Amen. *The concept for an Easter pageant, modeled on the new Christmas pageant, springs full-grown from my mind. I jot down the outline; I can't do more with it now; the baptism book is drawing me too irresistibly. Seeds planted long ago by* Piers Plowman *and the ECY liturgy are springing up and bearing fruit. After years of emptiness and fear, now joy, freedom, and love shower down on me. I am drowning in the Paschal mystery. I want to dance before the Lord; I want to sing and shout, to reach out my hands and lift others into the dance. Teaching, drawing, and writing, even making liturgy, are not enough—I want to preach; I want to lead; I want to open my heart and my hands and speak Christ in passionate love.*

The rector is leaving in May for a four-month sabbatical. During the summer, along with several others, I will be taking a turn leading the liturgy of the word and preaching. Before he leaves, I seek him out. "Thank you," I tell him, "for giving me so much rope over the last few years. Not everybody would have done that. Thank you for the chance to discover my gifts and my ministry." His reply is equally heartfelt: this is what his priesthood is all about; he has seen the change in me, and rejoices with me.

When he comes back, perhaps I will ask him to help me discern where my newfound sense of

· · · · · ·

vocation might be leading—how I can work more closely with him to make this parish a place where liturgy, celebration, and Christian education are one seamless whole; where God's people are made new and fed and filled with joy and live as a light to the world.

2

THE RECTOR left for his sabbatical on Ascension Day. He never came back. He and a young woman in the congregation had been carrying on an illicit affair, believing that in this accepting, inclusive parish such conduct would not be held against them. When they were discovered and confronted, they wove a web of lies; he himself lied to the bishop. As a staff member and the mother of his little girl's best friend, I unwittingly became part of the chain of events that led to his exposure and immediate removal. The parish plunged into utter devastation: he had been deeply admired and loved.

This business of forgiving him is a can of worms. I no longer want him as a friend, and, anyway, I will no longer be working with him: can you forgive somebody and make a breach with him at the same time? Can you be in charity with him and drop him socially at the same time? Does forgiveness bind one to a relationship that has lost its reason for being—just to fly one's flag, so to speak? What is the mark of forgiveness—how do you know you've done it—when your feelings about someone have permanently changed, because he has proved himself not to be the person you liked, the person you could trust and respect?

And how do you forgive someone who is not repentant?— who continues to say, "Isn't it too bad that this happened," instead of, "Oh my God, look what I did to all of you—I'm so sorry." I now see that the scriptural insistence on repentance is not so much a theological principle as a simple psychological truth: even God—especially God—cannot forgive wrongdoers who do not acknowledge the wrongness of what they have done. The ingredients for forgiveness are just not there.

But where does that leave us? Does God give us the same escape clause—the right to withhold forgiveness till the offender repents? The New Testament says no such thing. Can God forgive us for failing to forgive? Is "trying" to forgive (repenting for our failure to forgive—or at least, not resting content in our failure to forgive) acceptable, when forgiveness just won't come?

3

THE PARISH spent almost two years in transition following the rector's departure. The interim minister—the first woman priest the parish had ever known—was sensible, wise, and kind. But there was no quick fix for the grief and outrage, and then the exhaustion, which overtook the congregation and, for some, permanently damaged their capacity to find God in the institutional church. We had thought of ourselves as an exceptional community, a model of openness and reconciling love. Now we found that not only had our own pastor violated our trust, but we were not to be permitted to wrestle through our pain and anger directly with him, as many of us felt the gospel demanded. In accordance with diocesan policy, he was simply spirited away. Those who wished to confront him directly did so one by one.

Attendance fell off dramatically, especially among the newer members who had come to us as seekers or as refugees from spiritually oppressive environments. Many of these were the young parents. I found myself, in short order, with a near-empty Sunday school even though the children themselves were relatively untroubled by the rector's departure, since he had had little to do with children's programs. But if the parents dropped out, we lost the children, too. I called the families. It was always the same. "The kids really miss Sunday school," the parents would tell me. "They ask, 'When are we going back to church?' I know we should go back, but it just isn't the same without him." I listened, commiserated, exhorted, encouraged; but I could not make things better.

O God, God—why have you done this to us, to me? Why have you brought me out of exile and bondage, only to drive us all into the desert to wander in circles? Your people are lost and afraid, but I can't be their Moses; I'm not the priest, I'm not the pastor, I'm not the leader. I was ready, before this happened, to be Miriam: to walk with the leader, to lead the dance by the seashore in witness to your unfailing promise, your gift to us of freedom and new life. And for me, the pillar of fire still flames, but now no one else can see it; my time is out of joint. They are not ready to dance; I am compelled to stand aside while others, with different gifts, care for them in the way that they need. I am impatient, I am bursting with your fire: I can't wait. I need, how I need, for others to look up, to see that flaming pillar (how can they not see it?), to believe and rejoice that there will be water and manna, to take courage, to move forward. But my time is out of joint; and I'm not a pastor; I'm not a healer. You have called me to be something—maker, messenger, teacher, artist—it is these and more; but it has no name.

4

DURING THAT LONG INTERIM between rectors, I threw my energies into whatever creative work I could find or make. At church, The Christian Nurture Committee—three or four smart, generous, supportive parents and myself—determined to make the children's programming an island of celebration for ourselves and the handful of children who remained. Blending liturgy, learning, and play, we put the finishing touches on the cycle of seasonal celebrations that had been slowly evolving in the parish for almost ten years: "All Saints' Saturday," the Christmas pageant, "Palm Saturday," and now the Easter pageant. Presented on Low Sunday, this pageant was, in effect, lessons and carols for Easter, drawing its imagery from the Easter Vigil: creation, the dry bones, the Red Sea; bread, wine, water; cross, tomb, death, life. We—the small but spirited corps of children and adults who presented it—were so moved by what we had done that we looked around for a way to repeat it. I ran across a parish with an Ascension Day potluck supper and talked their rector (a friend of mine) into inviting us to do the pageant. *Hey, we are good*—and what we have to offer is *good news.*

At home, I threw myself into gardening till almost every square foot of our small yard was crammed with flowers and vegetables; I hung wallpaper and taught myself to quilt; I finished the baptism book, published a collection of Christmas pageant scripts, revised *The Sunday Paper* and began work on a second version, *The Sunday Paper Junior,* for younger children. And I began doing what Arnie called "moving and shaking" beyond the parish and my home business. I started a column in *The Living Church* on Christian education and children's spirituality, talked the diocese into paying my way to a distant conference, and enrolled in the diocesan parish development course to channel my energies into learning as well as creativity. It had become a matter of survival for me to understand the life of the gathered community. In the parish, I tried to work and to wait; I tried to stay within my job description; but I was too restless, too impatient. I kept pushing in where I had not been invited, and saying things better left unsaid.

The interim priest calls me into her office. "You're acting out," she says. "You have got to stop this acting out . . . but when the new rector arrives, you should start doing some serious thinking about whether you might be called to the priesthood."

I am chatting with the leader of the parish development class—a woman priest. She wants me to visit her parish to do some teacher training. Our conversation turns earnest, urgent, about what the Church really needs. She looks up at me from her chair. "Have you ever thought about ordination?"

I had been on the staff of a parish church for more than seven years; for fifteen years I had been immersed in teaching and liturgy—and it was not until I began to work closely with women clergy that a priest could look at me and see a potential leader and colleague instead of an intense, pious, somewhat unbalanced adolescent . . . a talented, unusually energetic Sunday school lady . . . or a pushy woman.

. . . . . .

I have found a spiritual director, a former seminarian with our parish, now ordained. We are talking about preaching, which I have now done two or three times. "It's terribly heady stuff," I say to her. "It's like nothing else; it feels utterly right. It's the one place where I am completely comfortable assuming authority with adults, where I don't worry at all what they think of me. What I am doing is not about me, or my authority: I am opening God's word to God's people; the authority is in the Word itself. It's a privilege and a gift . . ." My voice trails off. I look into her face. "I've known since I was ten years old that I'm called to preach."

Just after Easter, almost two years after the parish had plunged into crisis, we welcomed a new rector: a husband-and-wife team. By that fall, they had assembled a discernment committee for me, to begin exploring the possibility of ordination.

.

5

THERE ARE THINGS *that a lay minister cannot be. A lay minister can be a teacher, an artist—but (I see now) she hasn't got permission to dance. She isn't allowed to enter the magic world where it's OK to act in ways that aren't part of our culture—or rather, she can enter it herself, in private, but she hasn't got permission to lead others in. She is stubbornly particular; she has no tradition, no role, no name beyond her own name. She is herself, with whatever gifts God has given her; but she is not the sacrament of anything beyond herself. Maybe this is the inarticulate conviction behind many people's need to call priests "Father" or "Mother."*

I'm called not just to teach but to preach—and this is the difference between preaching and teaching: the preacher must also be a pastor, involved in people's lives with love and care, invited into people's lives with their own consent. Otherwise the preaching will become hollow and presumptuous.

But I've always said I'm "not a people person." I've even developed a theological rationale for it: in the image of the Trinity, I'm modeled on the Creator, not the Redeemer or the Sanctifier—I don't enter into others' lives to suffer and heal; I don't build bridges and inspire community; I just make things, and invite people to come and see.

But now I'm not so sure. If, in order to be a leader and a preacher, I will need to be a priest, then I must learn to love: to transpose my gifts into another key, to become schooled in the language of care, attention, and response. Listening, greeting, thanking; taking time from my projects simply to be present with others, remembering to call people who are in trouble, risking saying the wrong thing with people who are suffering; bringing people together and supporting them, encouraging them, challenging them. All these things that come naturally to other types of people: each of them is for me a bridgehead gained, a major undertaking.

This much I know: on that April day as I stood beside the cherry trees on the divinity school steps, God laid hands on me, overwhelmed all my questions, my fears, my anger, filled me with love and trust, set me on fire, and sent me out to preach and to lead. And that is that. And that fire has burned so brightly ever since that I can feel myself learning and stretching and beginning to have confidence that I can do well things that do not come naturally. But can I sustain it? How long will the fire burn?

. . . . .

PART NINE

Guide me, O thou great Jehovah,
pilgrim through this barren land.

1

ON THAT APRIL DAY when I had stood on the divinity school steps and felt my world change, I was thirty-four years old. Grace was six, and Margaret was just turning three. Arnie and I had talked about having a third child, but had postponed making a decision. We set my thirty-fifth birthday as an informal deadline to choose, yes or no.

We chose yes. This was arguably somewhat foolhardy, given the inner turmoil I was experiencing, and the vocational possibilities hovering on the horizon. But until the parish called a new rector, I could not move forward with my vocational quest, and I couldn't bear to be in a holding pattern about everything in my life. We had never had trouble conceiving, so I greeted each new month with tremulous excitement. But month after month, nothing happened.

I have made an appointment to see the doctor, just in case there is something to worry about. He finds nothing wrong; fertility simply declines with age. He suggests some simple interventions. "We can have you pregnant in a couple of months," he says. I am surprised at my own reaction: No thank you; I'd rather not. I have now become so caught up in my work and my spiritual drama that I no longer really want another child. But, I tell Arnie, I don't want to go back to using birth control, either. We decide not to decide; we go on as we have been doing: no birth control, no infertility treatments. And still nothing happens. Fine with me.

· · · · · ·

April again. I am now thirty-seven; our children are nine and six. For three years I have been straining to grasp, to name, to own the call from God, and to respond faithfully within the community of God's people. The desire and zeal have only grown stronger. My discernment committee has just recommended that I begin the process toward ordination.

This whole project is giving Arnie great distress. He is worried about the disruption and expense of my returning to school, when we have the children's education to plan for; he asks how I expect to keep up all my existing obligations and prepare for ordination besides. I don't know the answers; I'm still not sure, myself, that this is where I am called. That is, what I really want is the chance to keep on doing what I am doing now, at St. Paul's, with the added privileges of baptizing, celebrating the eucharist, and preaching. In my journal I rage helplessly against the canonical procedure that would require me to leave the community where my ministry was called forth (and where I have unfinished work, including my own children's spiritual formation), spend three years in seminary, emerge as a generic priest, an interchangeable part, and then enter a competitive job market where I would have to struggle, as a priest, to do the ministry I was already doing as a lay person before I started the whole process:

> I do *not* want to be ordained if it means stopping working with children. It's a double bind: if you want to work with children as a lay person, you are hampered by the low status of this ministry and your own low status as a lay person; if you want to work with them as a priest, you are stealing turf from one of the few bastions of lay ministry with any authenticity to it.
>
> But catechesis is, or should be, a priestly ministry. The clergy have usurped lay ministry in the world, by casting themselves as "professional Christians" and barging into the world's affairs as instant experts, "prophets," and moral agitators; they have usurped lay ministry in the

· · · · · ·

parish, by casting themselves as the only persons who are able to represent Christ; and they have abdicated their own most important role (after the liturgical one) which is that of catechesis, not only of adults but of children. The catechesis of children has become a lay ministry by default. It would be one thing for the priest to delegate this ministry to the laity, as the bishop delegates the ministry of baptism to the order of priests. But in general, clergy don't delegate it, they wash their hands of it.

How much do I try to live out a correction of this, and how much do I just go along with it so as to be able to do my work in the Church as it actually is?

In the second week of May, I flew to Cincinnati to conduct a workshop: my first out-of-state solo speaking engagement. The day after I came back, I discovered I was pregnant.

2

MY FIRST REACTION to the pregnancy was outrage and dismay: *what rotten timing!; I was just getting ready to leave everything in obedience to God's call and now he goes and changes the rules on me.* But along with the resistance there was pleasure and even a kind of relief. I struggled for about six weeks and then gave in to it—the strange, irresistible inwardness that always came with being pregnant.

I felt like a fool—I had persuaded all these people to take me seriously as someone with a vocation, and then I went and got pregnant on them, proving once again that it's just not worth giving time and energy to women, because what they really want to do is stay home and have babies. And I felt like a fool because it was true.

. . . . . .

My vocational quest simply shut down: I stopped writing in my journal; my prayer life collapsed; I found myself formulating my state of mind as, "If the phone rings and it's God, I'm not home." This midflight reversal, though not a complete surprise, was extraordinarily disorienting. I had assumed that the spiritual growth of the last three years would prove more substantial, more mature, less subject to almost instantaneous disintegration under an onslaught of hormones. But suddenly all I seemed to care about was sewing maternity clothes and looking for a bigger house. All I want to do when I am pregnant is *nest*.

Then, in early July, at eleven weeks, I miscarried.

Did I not want it after all? Did I somehow reject the pregnancy, and cause *the miscarriage? I feel as if I've simply been asleep or deluded for the last two months, and now I've come back to the real world, where we have two children, ages nine and six, and we've given away the crib and the playpen and moved on to other stuff . . . only now the difference is that I* mind. *I mind dreadfully. I am mourning my lost future as the mother of another baby; I'm mourning, with Arnie and the kids, the lost dream of a new member for our family; and I am also mourning my future as a priest, or even as a dynamic, creative lay minister, standing up in front of God's people and tossing out an inexhaustible supply of pictures of God.*

All the energy, all the commitment, all the vision of who I was and what I had to give to the Church are simply gone. They disappeared into thin air when I got pregnant, and now I'm not pregnant any more and they show absolutely no sign of coming back. I'm left with nothing, *except a lot of work that has lost all its meaning for me.*

■ ■ ■

Many people have said they are thinking of us and praying for us. But I don't feel supported by an invisible net of prayer. I feel totally alone and empty unless someone is actually with me, listening to me blather on or cry. "Thinking" about somebody doesn't make things better. Why should they care or appreciate that you're thinking about them? And if you are, why don't you call and tell them so?

· · · · · ·

Thank God for the ones who have stopped by with casseroles, or taken the kids, or put in time listening to me cry into the telephone. It's better to call for help than to tough it out; but it's best of all when the help comes unasked. I need to remember this for when others are hurting.

■ ■ ■

Three weeks have gone by; I have closed up; I am learning to be silent in the presence of the emptiness. Rather suddenly, during our (usually arid) family prayers, I begin to feel that perhaps the emptiness might somehow become the emptiness of Christ, who emptied himself; might become a kind of expectant (significant word!) emptiness, waiting to be filled by whatever God wants to fill it with: another baby, a renewed sense of vocation, something quite new and different . . . or maybe, for a while, simply a kind of clean, ascetic emptiness, like Lent:

> I said to my soul, be still, and wait without hope
> For hope would be hope for the wrong thing; wait without love
> For love would be love of the wrong thing; there is yet faith
> But the faith and the love and the hope are all in the waiting.
> Wait without thought, for you are not ready for thought:
> So the darkness shall be the light, and the stillness the dancing.

3

WE WENT AHEAD and bought the larger house we had been looking at before we lost the baby: we wanted something, at least, not to abort. We sold our first house to the owner of the restaurant next door. In November, right after we moved out, he bulldozed the entire garden and paved it over for a parking lot.

· · · · · ·

By Christmas, I was pregnant again. For the twelve days of Christmas, I walked around in a rapturous dream. All the Christmas Scriptures seemed written just for me: the exiles returning to Jerusalem, the Lord embracing them and tenderly leading them home. But on Epiphany I started to bleed. I was placed on bed rest in a vain attempt to fend off the inevitable: two weeks later, within a week of when the first baby was to have been born, I miscarried again.

I was worried about conceiving again; it never dawned on me I might conceive and then miscarry again. I was cherishing within me such a gift for everyone I loved; it was to be the answer to all our prayers. And now it's been yanked away—brutally, absurdly.

Arnie and the children seem to find this one less devastating than the first. It came and went so quickly, and they are so relieved to have me out of bed that the miscarriage is almost insignificant in comparison. I am finding, in fact, that people are inclined without thinking to treat the whole episode as an illness rather than a loss. While I was in bed, they called, offered to help, said they were praying for us; but now it's all over and I'm back walking around, they tell me how glad they are to see me again, as if now everything is fine. But it isn't. It's worse, much worse, than while I was out of circulation, socially "ill" but still clinging to hope.

I wish it wasn't winter. Then I could work in the garden. It's the only thing I can vaguely imagine myself getting interested in. Not that there isn't plenty to do; but I don't want to do any of it. I just want to stare at the wall, read, sleep, and cry. Most of all, I don't want to see anyone or go anywhere. I want to hide. I will simply have to disappear, somehow, because I can't bear being me, experiencing what I am experiencing. I had it; I had it back again, beyond hope, beyond belief; I had it—and now it's gone. Lent to Advent and then right back to Lent again.

There is no safety; there are no guarantees; there is no certainty, no time when you are "home free." Grace and Margaret were easily conceived, easily (more or less) born, and have led healthy, uneventful lives; but they are not "safe," and they never will be. God forbid, anything can happen. And just as I cannot protect them from harm, I cannot protect them from grief. Suffering is not a disease, that can be prevented by a vaccine or cured by an antibiotic. It's not something that, when it happens to you or to someone you love, you must run and find the "cure," and make everything normal again. C. S. Lewis says in A Grief Observed, *"Why can people not accept, that the only thing to do with suffering is to suffer it?"*

4

WE DID A BATTERY OF TESTS—everything normal. The doctors encouraged us to try again. We wanted that baby more than ever—we wanted desperately to come out of all this pain, frustration, and loss with something that would make it all seem to be worth while. On Mother's Day I was once again pregnant. We said nothing to the children, and we resolved that, for better or for worse, this would be our last try.

I wish I believed in magical prayer, but I just don't. I mean, God is there all right, and has something definite in mind, but I have absolutely no assurance that it coincides at any point with my wishes. So how does one pray? One simply says, "Here I am, this is what I want; and there you are, and I am choosing to trust you. I expect you to listen to me without mocking or belittling me . . . but I don't have any expectations that I can just put in an order and have it filled."

At eight weeks, we had scheduled an ultrasound, to enable us to relax, tell the children, and anticipate a real baby at last. Instead, the test showed a fetus that was two weeks too small, though it did have a heartbeat. They said I had my dates wrong, but I knew I didn't: for twelve months, my entire life had revolved around that calendar. Nervously, we waited two more weeks. A second ultrasound confirmed our worst fears. On the last day of school, just under a year after the first miscarriage, we had to tell the children that Mommy had been pregnant again and once again it had not worked. And we told them that we were not going to try any more.

Now I know how it goes: for the first couple of days, all you feel is relief that it's over—all the waiting, the worrying, and the whispering—the pregnancy, in retrospect, seems to have been so stressful that the end is almost welcome, just to be done with the suspense. Then, a few days later (when the kind phone calls begin to slack off, and people expect you to be up and functioning again, and you start to feel embarrassed to be constantly talking about it), the reality of what you had, and what you have lost, and the emptiness of the next days and weeks and months, all hits you like a ton of bricks and you start to go down, down, down into a really black and hopeless depression.

And nothing *seems interesting or important or worth bothering over; you have not only lost your hope of a baby, you have also, it seems, lost your whole sense of yourself, as someone with personality and interests, energy, and commitments. You feel you have just been* erased, *and what is left is a walking ghost or a kind of zombie, whose mind runs endlessly on one track while the world goes on around it. And you start to punish yourself because you know, in a way, you're not making any sense—if this is the kind of person you are, and the way the world seems to you, then the last thing you'd really be fit for is to take care of a real baby. Babies are hard work, and certainly not the answer to depression; babies grow and make more and more work and wear you out and cost a lot of money . . . and it seems so immature and stupid to go around acting as if the world is a blank and hopeless place, but if you just had a baby to take care of, everything would be hunky-dory. But that's the way you can't help feeling: nothing, but nothing, is right; but if you just had a little baby in your arms and it was* yours, *then everything* would be right . . .

. . . . . .

■ ■ ■

*I'm back to the "I never was pregnant; how could I ever have possibly believed I was pregnant?—
obviously it was all a big mistake" stage. It all seems totally unreal, even irrelevant, as if I'd thought
for a while that I had won the lottery. Except that I just can't get back to "normal." There's something
missing; whenever the phone rings I have this odd fantasy that it will be someone with good news—
"guess what, we found your baby"—as if I'd lost a dog or a cat, months ago, and there was still some
hope it might turn up.*

In a sense, ever since the whole quest for myself as priest, I've been pregnant with myself. *Have
I miscarried—or am I still pregnant?*

PART TEN

O love that triumphs over loss,
we bring our hearts before thy cross,
to finish thy salvation.

1

THE STRESS AND LOSS permeated the whole family, in a different way for each of us. For a while, Arnie and I were very angry with each other; he felt I was wallowing in self-pity; I felt he was being cold and heartless. Margaret, always a highly emotional child, responded to the three miscarriages (and a tornado that passed through New Haven three weeks later, bringing down eight huge oaks along our street, one of them barely missing our house) by developing severe nightmares and anxieties, about weather, separation from Mommy, and the deaths of everyone she loved. Grace kept her world controllable by establishing invariable routines for herself, and by reading, writing in her diary, and horseback riding.

We have developed a bedtime ritual to help calm Margaret's fears. It is based on compline and ends with the closing blessing:

> Guide us waking, O Lord, and guard us sleeping, that awake
> we may watch with Christ, and asleep we may rest in peace.
>
> *Parent*: Let us bless the Lord.
> *Child*: Thanks be to God.
> *Parent*: The almighty and merciful Lord, Father, Son, and Holy Spirit,
> bless us and keep us. Amen.

At the name of the Trinity, we sign a cross on her forehead. It does seem to help.

. . . . . .

■■■

I write in my journal a list of "Things I might do with the rest of my life":

- Write and illustrate children's books
- Get back to oil painting
- Teach elementary school
- Be a priest
- Get dissertation published and try to go somewhere with literature/theology
- Learn to play the piano well (probably impossible)
- Volunteer/work/organize in hospital/La Leche/Habitat/public schools/community gardening
- Figure out how to share my life in some way with kids that aren't mine

Interesting that "Christian education" isn't on here, except as subsumed in "be a priest," and "be a priest" is here mostly out of deference to its central place in the drama of the last several years. The whole business of churchiness just almost gives me the creeps right now, almost turns my stomach, makes me want to run the other way. I am either totally consumed by it or totally repelled by it. The most attractive things on the list are still the old inward-turning aesthetic ones . . . the very things I thought I was growing away from and out from.

■■■

Thank God I did not get ordained before all this happened. Imagine trying to live up to my own and everyone else's idea of what a priest should be, through all this struggle, pain, exhaustion, and depression. As it is, I can muddle through, doggedly get things done, in the parish as well as at home; but I cannot sustain the "learned behavior" of being emotionally available to others. I can be pastoral only when I am at the top of my form.

· · · · · ·

THE FIRST PART of myself to revive was the preaching. The clergy team at St. Paul's sched-uled me as an occasional preacher, and when I visited a parish or diocese as a guest speak-er I was also sometimes asked to preach. Always, it felt wonderful, and I knew that (what-ever my own doubts and conflicts) I had been given the gift of speaking the Word with truth and of offering it as *good news*. Often, people told me so; but even when they did not, I knew it.

The Sunday school once again began to grow. The new population was very different from the white, middle-class children who had flocked to us under the previous rector. The present rector couple had a child with special needs, and families whom they met in the course of his counseling and treatment began to turn up at church, bringing children with severe behavior and developmental problems and complicated medical conditions. A large family of foster children more than doubled our preschool population overnight. The cler-gy were generous mentors as I struggled to learn new ways of teaching, leading, disciplin-ing, and helping these children. In pageants and special presentations I began to focus on *loving* the kids rather than on *results*, and found, to my amazement, that when the relation-ships were right the results followed. I learned to relax into my work, and to give of myself; and the work began, ever so slowly, to feel like a vocation again.

Calling the roll for Christmas pageant rehearsals, I have learned to play master of ceremonies, introducing each participant and eliciting applause and cheers. When I call my own name, I look around in confusion. "She's not here," I lament. "She's never here! She misses every rehearsal!" "It's YOU!!" they all chorus, laughing and hooting. I do this every year now. The kids remember; it's become part of the tradition.

Simple stuff—you'd think I could do this kind of thing without even thinking. But I've had to learn, step by step.

· · · · · ·

I am preaching on All Saints' Sunday. Sunday school is canceled in honor of the feast; two dozen kids are sitting together on the floor at the front of the nave. From my lofty perch in the pulpit, before I begin my sermon, I stare them down, in the hope that they will be cowed into behaving themselves. Timmy, learning-disabled and uninhibited, catches my eye and winks.

Children draw pictures in church and give them to me at coffee hour. "I love God. I love you Gretchen."

3

JEANNE HAS COME TO OUR CONGREGATION *as a single mother, living alone with her youngest child, a nine-year-old with physical and developmental disabilities. She was a member of a charismatic church, where she was promised that prayer would save her marriage and heal her son. When this did not happen, she was blamed for her lack of faith. She is lonely and struggles with depression and many ghosts from her own childhood, but her faith is mature, tough, scriptural, and realistic. Her courage and resilience put me to shame.*

She stands in the hall outside the sanctuary, after church, in tears. She has been involved with a married man and has just discovered she is pregnant. She cannot bear to get an abortion: will we stand by her? Of course we will. On St. Francis's Day, three months after the last of my miscarriages, I am at Yale-New Haven Hospital, breathing with Jeanne through her contractions, holding her hands, staring into her eyes, counting, breathing, waiting. After nearly twenty-four hours of work, I watch as the baby is born; I hold him; I am his godmother.

■ ■ ■

We have planned our traditional Palm Saturday with the Sunday school children, in preparation for Holy Week: dramatized storytelling in the sanctuary, a variety of crafts and activities, a video after lunch. When we get up that morning, it is snowing. "No, we aren't canceling," I tell the worried par-

ents who call me at breakfast time; and by late morning the snow has stopped, the sun is shining, the sky is a warm, bright blue, and the fresh snow covering the little church garden is shrinking from the edges of the new green grass.

Our video is The Selfish Giant. *The giant's garden, locked in an endless winter, turns to springtime when he opens it to the village children. The very same transformation is happening right outside the parish house windows, as we watch. Angelica, a beautiful eight-year-old, is sitting on my lap, with her ten-year-old sister Jocelyn on the floor nearby. They are two of the eight foster children in one family. We are concerned about them: Sharon, the foster mother, is devoted to their baby sister, but cold and hostile to them, and has explained to us in their hearing that she only has them on account of the baby sister; they are adoptable but she wouldn't touch them with a ten-foot pole, and she fully expects them to end up pregnant, on drugs, in jail, or all three. They have visited several times at our house, to play with Grace and Margaret. Arnie knows I have thought of adopting them ourselves. It would be crazy, of course, and the state would almost certainly not place them with us anyway. But here with my arms around Angelica, watching the song sequence in* The Selfish Giant, *my eyes fill with hot tears:*

> Years go over, years go over,
> And the pleasures of the past
> Seem so empty, oh so empty,
> For I've learned to love at last.

4

HALFWAY UP THE STAIRS in our no-longer-quite-so-new house is the sweet little room that was to have been the baby's room. We have painted, wallpapered, and furnished it, because we have invited Miss Date to spend two weeks with us. Grace has met "Auntie Gwen" once, on a visit to England with her grandparents when she was eight. She remembers her English godmother as lively and easy to make friends with: well into her seventies now, Auntie Gwen still bicycles everywhere and takes a daily dip in the sea. The room has became "Auntie Gwen's room," and this is our way of saying goodbye to the hope of a baby, and reaching out to a different kind of love and hospitality.

The room is all ready; Grace, now eleven, has made the curtains herself. We are hurrying to leave for the airport; I am vacuuming the front hall; I pick up the day's mail off the floor and put it on the table without looking at it. At the airport, we watch all the passengers come through the gate. She isn't there. The children are frightened and upset. After a long chain of phone calls, we finally reach Miss Date's niece in England. "Didn't you get the telegram?" she asks. "She couldn't come; she had a heart attack two days ago." The telegram, in an envelope that looked like junk mail, was in the day's mail that I picked up off the floor. We drive home, two hours, with two sobbing children. The cycle of miscarriage continues: Auntie Gwen is recovering, but she will never be able to visit us.

■ ■ ■

Arnie and I have taken the exploratory course on adoption offered by the Department of Children and Youth Services. We are stuck: I really want Jocelyn and Angelica, but I know it would probably be disastrous for Margaret, whose own needs are very great right now. For a year I have been telling myself that this whole idea is only a fantasy, but today I have called DCYS for a report on their status. Their answer: Sharon has applied to adopt them.

She doesn't even like them—she's said so, a thousand times—but she won't let go of them, and DCYS has so far let her adopt every child they have given her. And what breaks my heart is to watch tough, brave, little Angelica reach out to Sharon because she needs a mother so badly . . . and all she gets is belittlement and brush-off.

The parish staff deliberated long and hard as to whether to intervene to try to stop the adoption, since the mother was so clearly emotionally abusing the two girls. Eventually we filed a report. All that happened, of course, was that Sharon withdrew her entire family from the parish, and the adoption went through as scheduled.

· · · · · ·

I have prayed and prayed for Jocelyn and Angelica, for Sharon, and for us. And here we are. Stuck: nobody able to break out of their neurotic myopia and build something that really will salvage these two brave little kids. God! God! Jesus! Get moving! *Do something!* For once, for once, come out with the mighty hand and the outstretched arm, instead of only the Cross, over and over and over!

■ ■ ■

Everybody I know has had miscarriages: aging "boomer" women who thought we had only to decide we wanted something and it would happen. But I am learning through a Bryn Mawr grapevine that progesterone seems to be effective after repeated losses similar to mine. I now have a niece and a goddaughter thanks to progesterone. My gynecologist almost gave it to me, that last time. If only he had.

■ ■ ■

We have known for some time that all is not well with the clergy couple who together serve as our rector. Now, on Palm Sunday, something is badly wrong; the wife has not returned from a trip out of town; nobody knows what is happening. On Maundy Thursday, at the liturgy, the senior warden reads a letter from the bishop explaining that she will not be returning. They are resigning as our rector. Easter is surreal: we are under water and can't seem to come up. Another crisis, another interim.

5

I AM FORTY; it's been six years since I began thinking about becoming a priest. It's not going to happen; the time has passed. We can't afford it, and anyway I still don't know if it's right for me. I've become an advocate for children in the church, and a teacher of teachers. I travel frequently to lead workshops and am writing a book for Cowley Press; I've been the primary drafter of the new Connecticut diocesan guidelines on Christian initiation and have accepted several writing assignments from the Office on Children's Ministries at the national church; I'm behind on deadlines and frantic because it's

· · · · · ·

spring and I can't find the time to work in my garden. The parish spirals downward into crisis; we are finally facing the disastrous extent of the deterioration in our huge old building.

The phone rings during a committee meeting with the new interim minister, at our house. Arnie's father has been taken to the hospital with congestive heart failure. He makes a partial recovery and goes home. We visit in June, at their place in Vermont where we have spent vacations for the children's entire lives. One of the reasons I married Arnie is that I could see what a fantastic grandpa Tony would be. In July, he and my mother-in-law take a long-planned trip to Europe, and in August, he and Arnie go to Boston for a Red Sox game. The following week, he collapses while walking up the pasture with a mechanic to work on the tractor, which had turned over, with him on it, several days before. Arnie and the kids, and Arnie's brother's family, are there on vacation when it happens; I was to join them the next day. The funeral is on Monday, the day after our anniversary.

I am numb; I have still not cried for him. I found out two weeks ago that I am pregnant. This was completely unplanned. I am taking progesterone; it's all I can think about.

■ ■ ■

THE PREGNANCY WAS UNEVENTFUL. Our third daughter, Marion, was born healthy on her due date, Maundy Thursday. We brought her home on Holy Saturday. Her Grandma, for whom she was named, was visiting for Easter.

We gather at the supper table; Arnie and the two big girls will be leaving after supper for the Easter Vigil. I light the candles. The baby is in my arms.

Mother:	Light and peace, in Jesus Christ our Lord.
Family:	Thanks be to God.
Mother:	Bless the Lord, who forgives all our sins;
Family:	His mercy endures for ever.
Mother:	Let us pray.

· · · · · ·

O God, Creator of heaven and earth: Grant that, as the crucified body of your dear Son was laid in the tomb and rest-
ed on this holy Sabbath, so we may await with him the
coming of the third day, and rise with him to newness of
life; who now lives and reigns with you and the Holy
Spirit, one God, for ever and ever. Amen.

*My voice breaks. Arnie blesses the food and we eat. Give thanks to the Lord, for he is good; his mercy
endures for ever.*

· · · · ·

· · · · · ·

PART ELEVEN

Come, labor on.
Claim the high calling angels cannot share—
to young and old the Gospel gladness bear:
redeem the time; the hours too swiftly fly.
The night draws nigh.

1

THE BABY'S BIRTH did bring healing, not only to me but to the family. She was an easy baby; she soaked up all the attention her sisters lavished on her, and grew and grew. All of us existed, for her whole first year, in a state of poignant joy and gratitude.

The parish, whose life was so intimately entwined with ours, began to move forward. A capital campaign raised the funds to repair the collapsing roof, and we called a new rector—a woman—under the rubric of "Restoring our Church, Renewing our Faith, Rebuilding our Community." We shored up our foundations by merging with a smaller, less viable parish that also felt called to remain in the city and work for diversity, justice, and wholeness.

I was ready, at last, to try again to find a name for who I was and what God had called me to do, and to see those wrapped presents that I had flung out in such numbers over so many years, as containing not only my *work*—my brains, energy, and creativity—but also my *self*—my capacity to learn, to love, and to give. "Learned behavior," still: but I had learned a lot. I even dared to hope that I had learned, finally, to love.

The parish needed to grow, to maintain and extend its diversity, to revive its heritage

· · · · · ·

of neighborhood outreach, especially with children, to forge connections between its food pantry ministry and its life of worship. I had created—over sixteen years and with the help of many parents, seminarians, and friends—liturgical celebrations with children that were stirring, compelling, and faithful to the gospel in all its complexity, as well as welcoming and fun; I had built a small but solid library of children's books; I had developed, tested, and refined storytelling techniques and materials. I had an articulate theology of offering the gospel to children; I had delved deeply, and often painfully, into my own childhood self, my own spiritual story and struggles; I had acquired some crucial tools for understanding how the faith community works and grows; and I knew what I wanted to build.

Shyly, tentatively at first, I told the new rector that I would be needing full-time employment to help pay for my children's education, and could she imagine me as a lay assistant? I told her I was ready to be, as I had once dreamed, a *missionary*; to hit the sidewalks and befriend the neighborhood kids; to show up every Saturday at the food pantry and start a story hour with the children waiting there with their parents for a bag of groceries; to design and lead an evening chapel service specifically for children that would bathe them in peace, comfort, and the assurance of God's love in the midst of a toxic and predatory world. I was ready, finally, to hear God's call clearly, and to say "Here I am"; to hear the words of the Sermon on the Mount without defensiveness and without excuses. I was ready to give everything I was, and everything I had learned. And, finally, I had a name for it: I was ready to be an *evangelist*.

2

A PARISH TASK FORCE *meets with a consultant and eventually endorses the establishment of the Children's Mission of St. Paul and St. James, under my leadership, subject to the obtaining of outside funding. Our timing is good. Children's ministries are gaining visibility and support in the church. We have articulated an exciting and innovative vision: grant money begins to flow in. The Mission job is part-time, till more funding becomes available, but I am working seven days a week; I'm still in charge of the Sunday school, and still running* The Sunday Paper *out of my home.*

We have called the evening chapel service Light *and* Peace; *it is based on compline and incorporates elements from my own family's evening prayers, including the bedtime blessing we devised for Margaret when she was frightened and could not go to sleep.*

We are planning the commissioning service, during the parish Sunday eucharist, that will inaugurate the Children's Mission. It will be adapted from the order for commissioning an evangelist in the Book of Occasional Services.

"Do you want me to lay hands on you?" the rector asks. "Do you want to stand, or kneel?"

"I think I want to kneel. And yes, I want laying on of hands."

■ ■ ■

Holy God, you have hidden your word from the wise of this world and revealed it to little ones. You have called us in the name of your Son to feed your lambs, and given us power by the Holy Spirit to bear witness to your love in every place. Be present with Gretchen as she goes forth in your Name. Let your love shine through her witness, so that the blind may see, the deaf hear, the lame walk, the dead be raised up, and the poor have the good news preached to them; through Jesus Christ our Lord. Amen.

■ ■ ■

. . . . . .

The words were extravagant, hyperbolic. Was it an ersatz ordination, as one member of the congregation commented (not unkindly)? I don't know. But at that moment, it felt absolutely right.

3

THE CHILDREN'S MISSION is four years old. It has not been easy: the children constantly challenge us with their woundedness, their boundless neediness; we are always scrambling to provide and sustain the infrastructure, the volunteers, leaders, advisors, and funding that a growing ministry must have. We have a summer program and are planning an afternoon program and ultimately a preschool; a dozen children have been baptized, but there is still a great gulf between Sunday morning and the Mission children, and we have not yet succeeded at involving the parents. As a pilot program, we are being closely watched, and this takes its toll: I struggle with anxiety, with fatigue, sometimes with near-burnout; God has seemed, too often, once again silent and inscrutable.

I know now that I will always have this struggle—that I am a leader, a teacher, a maker, but I am inexplicably called to a ministry the most essential feature of which does not come naturally to me. I am called, as I read in *Piers Plowman* long ago, to "lerne to love, and leef alle othere."

■ ■ ■

Summer program starts next week. I always have trouble at times like this, when the program itself is in recess and all I am doing is planning for the next program. I don't consciously miss the kids and the volunteers; in fact, consciously, I feel relief at being able to hole myself up with my program coordinator and do something with tangible, visible results—curriculum planning, fund raising, publicity, staff hiring—and to create order instead of mess in our program space and supply cabinet. But after a cou-

ple of weeks without the children, I find myself getting anxious and defensive. Will they ever come back? Is this whole enterprise completely unreal and scary and stupid? I find I'm terrified that it will all fall apart, nobody will show up, the volunteers will have a terrible experience, etc., and it will all be my fault. So this is when I have to get out and find the children and families and make it all seem real again.

For parish program, that means a phone sweep, to find out who's actually planning to come and who is planning to help. For mission program, though, at least a third of our families don't have phones, so it means getting in the car and going visiting. So there I am, a highly introverted intellectual, untrained in pastoral care or social work, calling on the urban poor in their homes.

The kids crowd to the door. They grab me around the waist and knees and hug me. "When does camp start? When can we come back?" I remind the parents of the registration deadline; I clear up a misunderstanding, pass on some useful information, hang out and chat for a while, and remind them, as I always do, that Sunday morning church is always in session. I need this; it makes me feel real again. And I know I have learned to do it well. I should do more of it—lots more. But there is always so much stuff that has to get done first.

4

TWENTY KIDS, a dozen adults (leaders and volunteers), and a meal-serving team from a suburban church are gathered in the chapel for Light and Peace. Tonight the kids have been having an unusually hard time settling down. They have repeated the rules together—"Raise your hand and wait your turn . . . Stay in your seat . . . Respect your neighbor"—but when the bell is rung and our adapted version of compline begins to fill the chapel with singing and prayer, many of the kids are still noisy and restless, competing for attention, invading each others' space, or simply tuned out. At one corner of the blue-and-white quilt where the children are sitting, eight-year-old Rayshawn is lying on his side in

· · · · · ·

a fetal position, sucking his thumb, with his coat pulled up over his head. He stays that way through the first part of the service, in spite of gentle attempts by a nearby volunteer to coax him out. Eventually, since he is not actually being disruptive, the volunteer lets him be. The rest of the kids gradually quiet down as the liturgy continues.

Tonight, the story is Jesus' Parable of the Good Samaritan. Just as the story is ending, Rayshawn peels back his coat from his face. Still lying on his side, gazing into space, he announces, "Sometimes, the least likely person turns out to be the hero." For the rest of the worship, and the rest of the evening—an art project in small age-based classes, and supper—he is alert, involved, and reasonably well behaved.

■ ■ ■

I'm at my desk, trying to finish a grant application. There's a knock on the door. It's Dawn and Darrell again. That's their picture, over my desk: the rector pouring water over Darrell's bent head, at the Easter Vigil two years ago. They came to us from the food pantry: they were two of our very first kids, nine and eleven years old, skinny and dirty, living with their drug-addicted mother in a boarded-up apartment with no electricity or running water, eating in soup kitchens. In the last four years, they have lived with their mother or their grandmother at at least six different addresses; they have each gone to three different schools. Dawn has run away from home and spent some time in a group home; Darrell has been arrested for shoplifting. Early on, we filed a report with the Department of Children and Families when we discovered that Darrell was being severely beaten by the grandmother. Repeatedly, we lost track of them. Repeatedly, they came back.

They want a ride home and a bag of food. They wanted the same thing two days ago, and last week. They walk to school, now, all the way across town; it's better than changing schools again after their latest change of address. Last year, their mother's kidneys failed; now she is virtually housebound except for twice-weekly trips to the hospital for dialysis. She is on the waiting list for a transplant. Her boyfriend is back in jail.

· · · · · ·

I invite them into my office. Dawn curls up on the couch with a picture book from the Sunday school book display. She is fifteen, taller than I am, big and bony. She asks when rehearsals will start for the Christmas pageant. The last time they were in it was three years ago. Dawn starts to sing: she remembers all the songs. Her eyes light up.

■ ■ ■

We tell the children, "God's love is always enough and more than enough." That is the Good News; and if we really believe it, what is there to fight over? What is there to be afraid of? I am called, as evangelist, to tell the story truthfully: to proclaim the gospel of abundance—the conviction, in faith, that God's love is enough—and never to confuse it with the false gospel of affluence—the arrogant assumption that God will provide for *me* but not necessarily for *you*. This too does not come easily for me. Perhaps this is why God has had to withdraw, again and again: to break me of my sense of immunity.

And we tell them, "Hear the story, and let it change you." The story has changed me, and it will continue to change me. It is not my gifts, my charisma, my brains, my spiritual stamina, that I have to offer the children. What I have to offer is simply the story itself, and the One it reveals—the One who emptied himself and yet remains ever full and overflowing—and the community of the faithful through which that story is patterned into our lives and given the power to live itself out as truth.

5

> You shall therefore lay up these words of mine in your heart . . . and
> you shall teach them to your children.
>
> —Deuteronomy 11:18–19

CHRISTMAS BREAK: *my kids are home from school, and I'm sitting at my desk trying to write, while the house vibrates with a recording of the latest Broadway blockbuster, played at full volume and considerably enhanced by the voices of six healthy teenagers, who have been "performing" it for each other all afternoon. The show,* Rent, *is about a group of struggling young artists and actors in Manhattan; the lyrics are explicit—sex, drugs, AIDS. The kids have brought their own costumes; they are trying to look hard-bitten and sophisticated. They are very serious about this project.*

After three hours of Rent *they come downstairs and eat an entire package of cookies, then go back up to top off the afternoon with a run-through of* Godspell. *Some of them were in a production of* Godspell *a couple of years back at the diocesan camp's Theater Week, and now one of them is planning to direct a concert production of it, apparently as a for-credit school project. The parents have their doubts about the feasibility of this, but the kids are full of confidence. I find myself stopping what I am doing, standing still in the downstairs hall, listening. They are singing "On the Willows," the poignant lament that comes just before the crucifixion scene. But they have changed it—there is a voice-over; it's Margaret's voice; as the others sing, she is reading: "He was despised and rejected, a man of sorrows and acquainted with grief . . . and the Lord has laid on him the iniquity of us all."*

It's a bare-faced borrowing from the comparable moment in our Easter pageant, which she has known since before she can remember. She's a chip off the old block. Suddenly my eyes are moist, my voice unsteady as I take four-year-old Marion upstairs for her bath. Now they have come to the finale. One kid has gone home but five others are jammed into the upstairs hall outside the bedroom where I am undressing the little one. The music on the tape is jangling and sinister, then eerily quiet.

. . . . . .

Oh God, I'm dying . . . Oh God, you're dying . . .
Oh God, I'm dead . . .
Oh God, you're dead . . .

They are all frozen in position, holding a long, sustained, high note. The doorbell rings. I leave Marion half-naked in her room and go down to let in the mother of one of the kids, who is here to take him home. She follows me upstairs. I've missed my favorite moment in the show, when the long sustained note breaks into the hushed and solemn strains of "Long Live God . . . Long Live God . . . ." They're already at the exuberant part, rocking to the beat, and when I go back into Marion's room she has taken off the rest of her clothes and is dancing naked on her bed. "Prepare ye the way of the Lord!"— she sings it perfectly—I have joined in with the counterpoint: "Long live God . . . "—we're singing together, dancing around her room:

Day by day, day by day, O dear Lord, three things I pray,
To see thee more clearly,
Love thee more dearly,
Follow thee more nearly, day by day by day by day . . .
Amen.